RESEARCH AND PRACTICE IN SOCIAL STUDIES SERIES

Wayne Journell, *Series Editor*

Teaching History for Justice:
Centering Activism in Students' Study of the Past
CHRISTOPHER C. MARTELL & KAYLENE M. STEVENS

Teaching History for Justice

Centering Activism in
Students' Study of the Past

Christopher C. Martell

Kaylene M. Stevens

TEACHERS COLLEGE PRESS

TEACHERS COLLEGE | COLUMBIA UNIVERSITY
NEW YORK AND LONDON

Published by Teachers College Press,® 1234 Amsterdam Avenue, New York, NY 10027

Copyright © 2021 by Teachers College, Columbia University

Front cover images: Student by MStudioImages / iStock by Getty Images; Angela Davis courtesy of the Library of Congress Prints and Photographs Division.

Library of Congress Cataloging-in-Publication Data is available at loc.gov

ISBN 978-0-8077-6474-9 (paper)
ISBN 978-0-8077-6475-6 (hardcover)
ISBN 978-0-8077-7926-2 (ebook)

Printed on acid-free paper
Manufactured in the United States of America

We dedicate this book to all the students we have taught and all the educators we have worked with. May they work for justice and be activists for change.

Contents

CHAPTER 1

Centering Justice in Students' Study of the Past

Oppression is interwoven into our histories. In the United States and globally, race, gender, class, sexual orientation, religion, and other social identities have long been used to create systems of advantage and to help certain groups maintain their power. In recent decades, this has been made more complex by the rise of populist nationalism and counterreactions to movements that seek equity for oppressed groups. In the United States alone, numerous recent historical events have highlighted persistent (and, in many cases, growing) social inequity: the Los Angeles Riots; the murder of Matthew Shepard and many other hate crimes targeting lesbian, gay, bisexual, transgender, and queer (LGBTQ) people; the treatment of Muslim Americans after September 11; the lack of care for Black and low-income people during and after Hurricane Katrina; the killing of numerous unarmed Black and Brown people, including Trayvon Martin, Michael Brown, Sandra Bland, Breonna Taylor, and George Floyd; the recent media exposure of the persistent gender discrimination and sexual abuse that women have faced in their workplaces and elsewhere; and the executive branch's targeting of Latinx immigrants and poor treatment of migrant families at the Mexican border. In response, several justice movements continue to organize and push for equity, including Occupy Wall Street, Black Lives Matter, and the Women's March.

Yet social systems have been designed on foundations of racism, sexism, classism, and other forms of supremacy, which make them almost invisible to those people with privilege. Despite the fact that recent illuminating events and powerful movements have captured the public's attention, most Americans who are in positions of power willingly or unwillingly choose to ignore our current social divisions. For instance, only 37% of White Americans feel that the country must go further in providing equal rights for people of color (Horowitz et al., 2019), only 42% of American men feel that more progress is needed in gender equality (Horowitz et al., 2017), and only 37% of middle- and upper-class Americans believe that advantages in life are the main factor in personal wealth (Dunn, 2018). Not surprisingly, in those same polls, the majorities of people of color, women, and people with lower incomes respond oppositely. Racism, sexism, classism, and other forms of oppression are maintained by the complicit, and often silent, benefiters of the system.

With this in mind, understanding the concept of inequity, how it functioned in the past (and has led to the present), and how movements of people have organized to create a more equitable society should be a main purpose of not only history education, but also education more broadly. Ultimately, education must be for liberation (Freire, 1970/2000; Lakey, 2004). We can rebuild our history classrooms to help students understand how citizens have formed movements to improve our society. We must give them the tools to understand how activists have done their work across history. In this book, we argue that classrooms should focus on teaching history for justice. In this chapter, we make the case for why it is needed, where it comes from, and what it looks like in practice.

WHY DO WE NEED TO TEACH HISTORY FOR JUSTICE?

A Need for Justice in Education

To prepare citizens to work against these persistent inequities built into every aspect of our society at the local, national, and global levels, our education system needs to center on justice. Schools, and especially history classrooms, should be places where students consider events, eras, and issues related to justice. While there are many different conceptions of social justice education, we work from a definition supplied by Ayers and colleagues (2009) that rests on three pillars:

1. *Equity:* The principle of fairness, which demands that what the most privileged are able to provide to their children (and receive for themselves) must be the standard for all, and that there must be a redressing and repairing of historical and embedded injustices.
2. *Activism:* The principle of agency, which involves a full participation, preparing students to see, understand, and, when necessary, change all before them.
3. *Social Literacy:* The principle of relevance, which involves resisting the effects of materialism and consumerism, as well as resisting the power of social evils rooted in forms of supremacy (i.e., White supremacy, patriarchy, homophobia), and nourishing our awareness of our own identities and our connections with others, and how our lives are negotiated within preestablished power relationships.

Ayers and colleagues argued that social justice education ultimately embraces the "three Rs" of relevant, rigorous, and revolutionary. It involves a curriculum connected to the lives and cultures of the students. It involves setting high academic standards for all students with embedded support and care to help them reach those standards. It involves a positive transformation of students' lives and their communities, but also a rethinking of the larger social order.

Ladson-Billings (2015) recently argued that we must replace the term "social justice" with "just justice" to describe our collective work in making the world fairer. She argues that the difference is not only a semantic one, but also a fundamental rethinking of our task as human beings. The term social justice is not expansive enough to help us confront the injustice that permeates all aspects of our society. Ladson-Billings built her reasoning on four main contentions: (1) Social justice has become oversimplified into a buzzword; it may be used due to its fashionableness and without a deeper understanding of inequity and how it works (and how it can be undone). (2) Social justice has become part of a discourse of "can't" or a deficit view of students, especially students of color or poor students. (3) Social justice has become a political target, especially for those on the far right, labeling it purely as ideological and lacking any substance. (4) Social justice is too narrow, and we lose sight of the big picture and the injustice that prevails across the country and around the world. For these reasons, we also choose to be more intentional in our language, and throughout this book we use the word "justice," just justice, to describe what we hope students and teachers will focus on in their work.

Finally, we also acknowledge that any justice work must lead with race. While students must also investigate issues of sexism, classism, nativism, cisheterosexism, and homophobia, they would benefit from understanding that race has long served as the main social dividing line and that all forms of oppression must be considered in intersectional ways (including how they intersect with racism) (Crenshaw, 1991; Davis, 1981). Ultimately, if we are able to dismantle racist systems that govern our world, it will help aid in dismantling all systems of oppression (as all systems of oppression are connected) and liberate all. Only then will we have a legitimate democracy (Davis, 2011, 2016). As such, throughout this book, we intentionally choose to forefront race and racism in our discussions of justice. As Brown and Brown (2011) remind us, "race—perhaps more than any other sociocultural factor—is the most challenging and complex to understand" (p. 9), and that justice work must critically engage with issues of race and racism, as it "sets the stage for preparing students to believe in and act in the interest of social justice" (p. 10). We work from Kendi's (2019) definition of racism as "a marriage of racist policies and racist ideas that produces and normalizes racial inequities" (pp. 17–18), as it very explicitly explains racism in terms of inequity, rather than discrimination (which has been used to prevent attempts at making systemic social change). Our leading with race and racism is not to underscore the importance for students to learn about other forms of oppression. Rather, race and racism can offer a road map for understanding how oppression operates broadly, how it can function differently in relation to other social identities, and, ultimately, how it can help push us to better work for justice in all aspects of our society.

A Need for Justice in Theory and Practice

There is justice in theory, and there is justice in practice; the two must work in tandem. We will never have a fair and equitable society without theories to guide the work of justice or without people on the ground organizing movements for justice. If we look at some of the most successful justice movements over the past century, from the labor movement to the civil rights movement or anti-war movements, they were successful as a result of both the theories and practices of their members.

Much of the current thinking on justice comes from a Eurocentric perspective and is rooted in the work of Rawls (1971/1999). In his concept of distributive justice, he argued,

> Justice is the first virtue of social institutions, as truth is of systems of thought. A theory however elegant and economical must be rejected or revised if it is untrue; likewise laws and institutions no matter how efficient and well-arranged must be reformed or abolished if they are unjust. (p. 3)

At the most basic level, Rawls (1991) argued that justice is fairness. It is a moral, political, social, and economic principle. It is the major foundation of democracy and the institutions that support democracy. He argued that at its core was an attempt to reform societies around liberty and equality.

Rawls's (1991) work was built on centuries (perhaps millennia) of European philosophical scholarship related to justice. Plato defined justice as being the virtue of society as a whole, which directly related to the unequal relations between people (Jackson, 2005). Rawls built his own work on Aristotle's definition of distributive justice (Jackson, 2005). Granted, modern conceptions of justice are substantially different than these classical notions (e.g., Aristotle was concerned more with political power, rather than economic distribution).

In Europe, the Middle East, and Latin America, the concept of justice has also had a religious element. Several religious groups have developed faith-based conceptions of justice. For instance, the Roman Catholic Church has long had language in its guiding documents around social justice, including its teachings on human solidarity. More recently, the Catholic Church has made explicit statements on social equity and justice, including, "Society ensures social justice when it provides the conditions that allow associations or individuals to obtain what is their due, according to their nature and their vocation" (Catholic Church, 1994, p. 468). It is within this Catholic tradition that the concept of liberation theology was born in Latin America in the 20th century (Gutiérrez, 1988), which directly emphasized liberation from oppression as an important component of Christian beliefs. The concept of social justice has also been a significant component of the Jewish and Muslim faiths. While Judaism and Islam frame the concept around their individual religious tenets, both share an emphasis on basic human rights, collective well-being, and the general welfare of people (Accomazzo et al., 2013). Broadly, these concepts of justice are rooted in attempts to create fairer communities and societies.

Ladson-Billings (2015) argued that, while Rawls's (1971/1999) work is important, we must shift our understanding of justice away from Eurocentric views, as they overly focus on established social institutions. According to Sen (2009), and based on Indian conceptions, justice is not simply related to institutions, but more importantly it is "ultimately connected to the way people's lives go" (p. x). This view involves *niti*, or the strict organization and behavioral rules for justice, and *nyaya*, or the larger picture of how those rules affect ordinary people's lives. If we focus our quest for justice solely on creating just institutions, then we may lose sight of the ultimate (and perhaps more immediately important) goal of improving people's lives. Additionally, Elechi (2004) outlined an African indigenous perspective of justice (which had been displaced by European colonial views) that is built on restorative and transformative principles, where "victims, offenders and the entire community are involved and participate in the definition of harm and search for resolution acceptable to all stakeholders" (p. 1). We root our understandings of justice, and history for justice, in these conceptions of justice.

Justice does not happen on its own; it requires a practice that includes discussion or consciousness raising, organizing, and collective action. In their book on how to organize civil rights movements, Oppenheimer and Lakey (1965) argued that democratic movements could only be successful when their members understand effective tactics and are educated to use those tactics. Citizens are not typically educated in ways to examine a "complicated piece of social machinery . . . and some of the levers which can be used to bring about change" (p. xii). In part, because social institutions are often built to maintain the status quo (and prevent change), our education system has not generally prioritized consciousness raising, organizing, or taking action for social change.

If the purpose of school is to prepare and foster democratic life (which in our current age is certainly, and incorrectly, being contested by some), then we must teach citizens how to do the work of democracy; we must teach students how to use the levers of the social machinery. Social change requires movement building and sustained civic effort both inside and outside established political systems. Skillful advocates know how to use an array of tools within a democratic toolkit. If our education system does not provide these tools, citizens will be left to develop them on their own (which may be possible, but likely less successful); or, more likely, citizens will continue to have growing frustration and apathy toward democracy. We are observing this phenomenon in many democratic nations around the world (including the United States), with an increasing number of citizens supporting authoritarianism (Drutman et al., 2018; Foa & Mounk, 2016; Levitsky & Ziblatt, 2018).

Students demand an education system that prepares them to change the world and teachers that can support them in that endeavor. Teachers can enact what Love (2019) called abolitionist teaching or "a way of life, a way of seeing the world, and a way of taking action against injustice" (p. 89). As Love argued, there is no one way to be an abolitionist teacher, but at its core, it is teachers working in solidarity with their students and school communities to center freedom and uplifting humanity in all decisions. This involves listening and sometimes following the students. As Ayers and colleagues (2009) contended, "Sometimes students lead the way, and wide-awake teachers—students of their students—can learn a thing or two about courage and integrity" (p. 728). And they are learning; in recent years, students have been key organizers of many movements, including Black Lives Matter, the pro-gun-control March for Our Lives, and the global School Strike for the Climate. Students in these movements are justice-oriented citizens, which Westheimer (2015) described as citizens who are "able to think about issues of fairness, equality of opportunity, and democratic engagement . . . [and are] thoughtfully informed about a variety of complex social issues, think independently, and look for ways to improve society" (p. 40).

This is an opportune time to refocus schooling on democratic values and on helping prepare students to do the work of democracy. With major world challenges such as growing inequity and global warming, now more than ever, we need an education system that can prepare students to take democratic action. As Zinn (1997/2009) argued, "The road from study to action is short" (p. 572). As a result, our education system is crucial in

> bring[ing] teachers and students together, not through the artificial sieve of certification and examination but on the basis of their common attraction to an exciting social goal . . . accepting as an educational goal that we want better human beings in the rising generation than we had in the last [and] requir[ing] a forthright declaration that the educational process cherishes equality, justice, compassion and world brotherhood. (p. 572)

Education must provide the tools necessary for students to engage in civic problem solving and reenvision society for the better.

At the same time, the role of education should be to link the theories and practices of justice, so that students can both understand what justice is (and how there are different conceptions of it) and learn how to do the work of justice in the real world. Too often, education for justice has taught students about justice in concept, but it has not given them the tools needed to engage in the work of justice. This book aims to bridge the theory with the practice of justice. It intends to explain how conceptual work and research on justice can look inside and outside the school, and specifically the history classroom.

A Need for Justice in History Education

In his widely read piece for the American Historical Association, Stearns (1998) argued that the reasons for studying history are that, as a school discipline, it:

1. Offers a storehouse of information about how people and societies behave.
2. Leads to understanding how the past caused the present, and so the future.
3. Adds perspective on our own lives related to human life and society.
4. Provides a terrain for moral contemplation.
5. Helps provide identity.
6. Is essential for developing good citizenship.

We contend that the main idea overarching Stearns's list is that the study of history is ultimately to make the world better. We must understand our past to ensure we make informed decisions in the present and future. Most of the problems our world will face over the next century will be caused or exacerbated by social inequity; to be prepared as democratic citizens* to grapple with those issues, students must learn how to be critical interpreters of the past.

Over the past two decades, scholars have argued that the history classroom, and by extension history teacher education, should center on inquiry as it relates to historical thinking (Martin & Monte-Sano, 2008; VanSledright, 2011; Wineburg, 2001) and democratic citizenship skills (Barton & Levstik, 2004; Grant et al., 2017; Lévesque, 2008). Without a doubt, it is incredibly important to understand the nature of the discipline and how historians construct the past, and it is also important to learn how to use history to inform democratic decisions in the present. While these two types of thinking can help students address the larger issues of justice in society, they do not always make it the focus of learning. As such, we argue that "thinking

---

*Throughout this volume, we use "citizens" broadly to include all members within local, national, or global communities with civic responsibility, regardless of their state-determined citizenship status, which often excludes documented and undocumented immigrants, as well as members of politically marginalized groups.

like an activist" is an essential third perspective missing in history education. Through an activist lens, the study of history can help prepare students
and citizens to be society's needed change agents. Moreover, the shift that
we are arguing for in school history is aligned with recent shifts in academic
history. In fact, some of the most important academic works of history over
the past half-century have examined the past through a justice-view (e.g.,
we think of the work of Howard Zinn, Laurel Thatcher Ulrich, Ibram X.
Kendi, Eric Foner, and Tamim Ansary). These academic historians leveraged
their historical, democratic citizenship and activist thinking to interpret the
past and impact how we understand the present and future.

WHERE DOES TEACHING HISTORY FOR JUSTICE ORIGINATE?

Fostering Activism in the Study of the Past

History education is an important vehicle for teaching students how activism was used in the past to improve society, for connecting those movements for justice to today, and for envisioning ways that students may use
similar democratic tools to change society in the present and future. As
Moyer and colleagues (2001) have argued, social movements have long offered road maps for citizenship and social change, and they should comprise
the main lens through which we read history. They wrote,

> Throughout much of human history, people have organized to change social
> conditions. Some collective efforts have had dramatic success, while others have
> failed miserably. Nonetheless, the advancement of human society has largely
> been achieved through citizen-based actions. In the United States, the recognition
> of basic human rights—the abolition of slavery, the right of labor to organize,
> child labor laws, the right for African Americans and women to vote—came
> about through the efforts of engaged citizens. In recent years, activists around
> the world have ousted dictators in Eastern Europe, the Philippines, and Haiti
> and ended apartheid in South Africa. Nonviolent social movements, based in
> grassroots "people power," are the means for ordinary people to act on their
> deepest values and successfully challenge unjust social conditions and policies,
> despite the determined resistance of entrenched private and public power. (p. 1)

As we noted earlier, historians have long written about the past to help
us understand how our current society came to be, and this should be the
main goal for students. Moreover, public education has long had a goal of
fostering social change and civic virtue; for instance, they were major values
guiding Horace Mann's vision of common schools and the education reforms of the Progressive Era. To prepare students to be agents of change in
the present and future, students need to learn how to think like activists in

their history classrooms. To support this, we outline two frameworks that were created by civil rights activists to help others build movements, and we suggest that teachers use these frameworks to help students analyze and understand the past (which we will elaborate on in Chapter 2).

In the mid-1960s, Oppenheimer and Lakey (1965) created their "manual for direct action" to explain how the civil rights movement was built over time, was intentional in its strategies, and can be a model for other social movements. This work was the inspiration for a framework that Lakey (2004) later created, which he dubbed "strategies for living a revolution." He argued that there are generally five stages of any successful social movement: cultural preparation, organization building, confrontation, mass political and economic noncooperation, and parallel institutions. Moreover, social movements often fail at one of these stages, so Lakey offered ways to overcome potential movement pitfalls. As such, he made the case that this framework could be used to understand not only how a successful movement was built, but also how unsuccessful movements failed.

In the 1980s, based on their decades of social activism, Moyer and colleagues (2001) created the Movement Action Plan (MAP) to describe the eight stages that social movements use to influence progress and achieve positive social change: (1) status quo, (2) normal channels fail, (3) conditions ripen, (4) take off, (5) perception of failure, (6) win public support, (7) success, and (8) continuation. They group these eight stages into four periods: steady state (stage 1), buildup of stress in the system (stages 2–4), seen as a general problem (stages 5–6), and resolution (stages 7–8). Much like Lakey (2004), Moyer and colleagues (2001) made the case that their framework could also be used to understand how movements were successfully built, as well as used as a tool to understand how other movements failed.

Thinking Like an Activist Framework

While Lakey's (2004) and Moyer and colleagues' (2001) frameworks offer slightly different descriptions of the stages that successful social movements include, there is a significant overlap. As a result, we use them jointly as the foundation for our "thinking like an activist" framework. We argue that thinking like an activist comprises three main components: (1) cultural preparation, (2) critical analysis, and (3) collective action. Students should use these three concepts (and related questions) to analyze events in the past (or present):

- Cultural preparation involves creating a new vision of what society can be instead of the status quo; it involves unlearning oppressive structures and building solidarity. Did a group of people at the time want to change society, and did they have a vision for how it might look different? If so, what was that vision and how was it different?

- Critical analysis, or developing sociopolitical consciousness, is the ability to recognize how oppression is constructed and how power structures are replicated. Did a group of people at the time outline and help educate the public about a particular type of oppression and ways that they could work against it? Did they make the case to the public that alternatives to the status quo would benefit all?
- Collective action is the work of activists; it is how movements enact change. Did a group of people at the time engage in collective action? (Was there a "trigger event" that gained public attention? What methods were used to raise public awareness?) Did the movement gain public support? Did the groups' collective actions lead to a resolution and change in society?

Since these components generally describe what successful social movements include, we argue that they can provide helpful tools for students to analyze past events. These three components (cultural preparation, critical analysis, and collective action) can be used to analyze any historical event. From the American Revolution to the Yellow Turban Rebellion in Han China, from the Industrial Revolution to the postcolonial African independent movements (which provide more examples in Chapter 2), students should be engaged in various classroom activities that keep coming back to this framework.

Using the Civil Rights Movement to Understand Activism

To illustrate how a historical event could be analyzed using the "thinking like an activist" framework, we will use the modern civil rights movement. We use this for three reasons: First, the modern civil rights movement is a widely taught topic in American schools, and it is often included at various levels from elementary school to the university, so most students and people will have knowledge of it. Second, it is a prime example of a long-term and successful movement of activists. It was complex and involved many different perspectives, yet all were focused on ending racial segregation and providing justice for all Americans. Third, it is the social movement that was the inspiration for Lakey's (2004) and Moyer and colleagues' (2001) frameworks.

When students approach the civil rights movement using this framework, they would first ask about cultural preparation. They may conclude that starting as far back as the end of slavery (or perhaps earlier with the abolitionist movement), a group of people led by African Americans themselves envisioned a society where Black people had equal rights in all facets of life, including voting, employment, housing, and public services (such as education and health care). This vision was quite different than the status quo that relegated Black people to a second-class citizenship status and in most places a de jure or de facto segregation. Next, the students would determine if the movement had developed a critical analysis of the situation. They may decide that there is strong evidence to argue that it did, as numerous Black scholars, including Frederick Douglass, W. E. B. Du Bois, and Carter Woodson, laid their groundwork for understanding how racism and segregation worked. This was followed by legal, political, and moral cases made by the National Association for the Advancement of Colored People (NAACP), Southern Christian Leadership Conference (SCLC), Student Nonviolent Coordinating Committee (SNCC), Congress of Racial Equality (CORE), the Nation of Islam (NOI), Organization of Afro-American Unity (OAAU), and the Black Panther Party (BPP), where these groups made public arguments against the status quo. They used a series of actions, such as organizing, lawsuits, protests, rallies, lobbying, and education campaigns, to change the public's perceptions (including those people who held power and attempted to defend the status quo). They offered alternatives to how society may look if it were built on equity. While different parts of the movement proposed different solutions—for instance, the NAACP and SCLC generally focused on integration, while the BPP, NOI, and OAAU focused more on self-determination and Black nationalism (and SNCC and CORE had members in both camps)—they all pushed the public to consider a future without discrimination and segregation. Last, the students would ask how the movement engaged in collective actions. They may claim that there was a "trigger event," such as the murder of Emmett Till or the attempted integration of Little Rock Central High School, which forced the public's attention on the issue. They may argue that sit-ins, marches, or massive rallies helped gain support for the movement. They may debate whether nonviolence or "by any means necessary" was a better strategy. Finally, they would have to make a concluding determination as to the overall success of the movement and if it changed society (which most would conclude that it did).

HOW DO WE TEACH HISTORY FOR JUSTICE?

Using a Pedagogy of History for Justice

Based on these principles of activism and the growing body of research, we argue that history classrooms built around "history for justice" will include three main pedagogical approaches: social inquiry, critical multiculturalism, and transformative citizenship. First, to foster students' critical analysis, history teachers should create opportunities for students to investigate the past using social inquiries. Second, to develop students' cultural preparation, history teachers should design the curriculum to be both critical and multicultural. Third, to teach students ways that they can participate in collective

Figure 1.1. History for Justice Framework

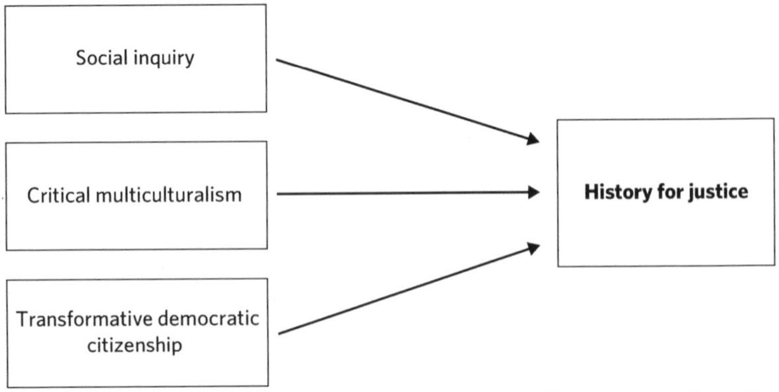

action, history learning communities should be built around fostering transformative democratic citizenship. Figure 1.1 highlights how these three
ideas feed into a larger conception of history for justice pedagogy. We will
then elaborate on each of the three assertions and connect them in the preexisting literature on justice in social studies education.

Social Inquiry

Inquiry is how humans understand the world around them. Barton and
Levstik (2004) defined historical inquiry as a process involving "asking questions, gathering and evaluating relevant evidence, and reaching conclusions
based on that evidence" (p. 188). A basic definition of the word "social" is
"of or relating to human society, the interaction of the individual and the
group, or the welfare of human beings as members of society" (Merriam-
Webster, 2019). With this definition in mind, we suggest that we add social to
the inquiries that we use in the history classroom, because the core purpose
must be to ask questions and gather and evaluate evidence through the lens
of power relationships in the past, which has led to the current present and
influences our future (similar to what others have labeled critical inquiries).
It is important to understand the welfare of human beings in a society over
time and how equity has or has not been present in those societies.

  If inquiry is to be a tool for justice, it must specifically engage in social
inquiries (which is the concept explored in Chapter 3). As Salinas and
Blevins (2014) reminded us, inquiries can be about any topic and, in themselves, do not have to focus on inequity or power relationships. Instead, they
advocated for the use of "inquiry as a means of troubling, complicating,
countering or resisting narratives that marginalize or omit others from the
telling of history" (p. 36). Martell (2018) similarly described inquiries as:

"Challeng[ing] students to specifically think about how past events contributed to their lives and society, learn[ing] not only their own histories but also the histories of others, and examin[ing] past inequity and its relationship to present inequity and possible solutions. (p. 64)

Moreover, Santiago (2019) described three key ways that history class-rooms can foster this:

(a) the experiences of people of color [and other social groups that face oppression] cannot be essentialized, (b) inquiry can be a useful tool in encouraging historical reasoning that considers such racial/ethnic [gender, class, sexual orientation, etc.] nuance, and (c) collective memory might be leveraged to encourage students to develop such relational analysis. (p. 114)

By the questions they ask and the sources they use, teachers may be intentionally or unintentionally transmitting historical narratives and collective memories and using narrative templates that represent the perspective of dominant groups. They may be selecting sources that represent the perspectives of the groups that maintain power. Instead, inquiries must be critical and facilitate a contested space to uncover and confront inconsistencies in the historical record and reveal voices that were often intentionally silenced or erased from the historical record.

Critical Multiculturalism

As a nation, the United States is becoming more diverse. Although the United States has always had racial, class, gender, and cultural diversity, American society has never truly acknowledged its multiculturalism. Even worse, it has obscured how oppression based on race and culture has been at the core of our society's foundation (Banks, 2004; Ladson-Billings, 2003). In social studies, this is manifested through a curriculum that presents history through the lens of White history, where race is invisible and White experiences are predominant (Chandler & Branscombe, 2015). At the same time, the history curriculum maintains male, middle-class and wealthy, and heteronormative views of the past (Au, 2009; Crocco, 2001; Mayo, 2007; Noddings, 2001). In most history classrooms, racism is only discussed in a handful of learning units, such as European colonization, slavery, or the modern civil rights movement. Similarly, sexism and classism may be only discussed when the history curriculum covers women's rights (such as suffrage or women's liberation) and industrialism and unionism (such as turn of the 20th century Europe or the United States), respectively, and the curriculum may never cover the rights of LGBTQ people. At the same time, when race, gender, class, and sexual orientation are presented in the curriculum, they are usually presented through a tolerance-oriented lens (Martell, 2017; Martell & Stevens, 2017b) or through liberal multiculturalism (May & Sleeter, 2010), where the focus is on groups getting along better through the acknowledgment of differences, rather than acknowledging and trying to correct systemic inequity.

If the curriculum is to be a tool for justice, it must present a critical multicultural perspective (which is the concept examined in Chapter 4). Where liberal multiculturalism primarily focuses on acknowledging and respecting differences, critical multiculturalism "gives priority to structural analysis of unequal power relationships, analyzing the role of institutional inequities, including, but not necessarily limited to racism" (May & Sleeter, 2010, p. 10), and it helps teachers develop equity-oriented stances, focusing on the creation and maintenance of systems of advantage (Martell, 2017; Martell & Stevens, 2017b). The curriculum must not only include multicultural voices and perspectives, but also center multicultural understanding on how racism, sexism, classism, cisheterosexism and homophobia, and other forms of oppression and discrimination have influenced history and have led us to the present and envision a different future. It requires teachers having thoughtful considerations of whose voices are and are not included in the curriculum, and when underrepresented groups are included, if their representation is accurate and authentic (Busey, 2014; Busey & Cruz, 2015; King, 2016; King, Davis, & Brown, 2012; King et al., 2014; King & Womac, 2014; King & Woodson, 2017; Rodríguez, 2018; Santiago, 2017; Woodson, 2015, 2016). The "add diversity and stir" view of history, as Noddings (2001) called it, must be replaced with an embedded fairness view of history, where students will focus their analysis on equity (or the lack thereof) across all lessons.

Transformative Democratic Citizenship

If the ultimate purpose of schooling is to prepare citizens for democratic life, history education should also contribute to this end. Yet we know that dominant groups often use democracy to protect their political and economic power (and will sometimes curtail democracy, when marginalized groups demand rights or unite with others to gain political strength), and we know that history education has often been used to justify the status quo and uphold current power arrangements (Banks, 2004; Ladson-Billings, 2003). Relatedly, Banks (2017) described a failed citizenship as the following:

> when individuals or groups who are born within a nation or migrate to it and live within it for an extended period of time do not internalize the values and ethos of the nation-state, feel structurally excluded within it, and have highly ambivalent feeling toward it. (p. 367)

He argued that schools (and their history classrooms) contribute to this failed citizenship when they use "assimilationist approaches to civic education that requir[e] minoritized students from diverse groups to deny their home cultures and languages" (p. 367). Teaching the past from the dominant lenses perpetuates the status quo; furthermore, it teaches students to assimilate, which continues to marginalize and alienate students of color, as well as women, queer, immigrant, and poor and working-class students. Instead, the purpose of social studies should be to help students sustain their cultures (Paris, 2012; Paris & Alim, 2014, 2017).

If learning communities, including the history classroom, are to be tools for justice, they should be built around fostering a transformative democratic citizenship (which is the concept discussed in Chapter 5). As Lévesque (2008) has argued, history education "can make an important contribution to democratic citizenship. Historical knowledge of political, social, cultural, and economic systems overlap[s] with the democratic knowledge necessary for active citizenship . . . [and to] more effectively engage in democratic society" (p. 28). Aligned with this idea, Banks (2017) argued that history teaching must "help students from marginalized groups become recognized and participatory citizens by attaining a sense of structural integration and inclusion within their nation-states and clarified national identities" (p. 373). History classrooms must be places that help students develop a sociopolitical consciousness and cultural competence, which are essential citizenship skills in any multicultural state and globally (Ladson-Billings, 1995a, 1995b, 2006, 2014), and a place to help students, especially students of color, define, redefine, and sustain their cultures (Ladson-Billings, 2014; Paris, 2012; Paris & Alim, 2017). Within history classrooms, learning communities should be focused on understanding how citizenship has been denied to many, with the goal to create a democracy that is open to all and based on principles of justice. It should model democratic ideas and practices, and it should be a place for students to engage in active citizenship.

CONCLUSION

The power of democracy is its adaptability to a changing world. We can envision and work toward a society that is more just than the present. History education is more relevant now than ever. The problem is that the way it has been traditionally taught, as the recall of facts or the memorization of names, dates, and places, has not been the tool that citizens need to make our society better. We hope this book offers ideas and strategies that can transform the history classroom into a space for understanding the past with the explicit purpose of learning from past movements for justice and building future movements that restore a faith in democracy.

CHAPTER 2

Thinking Like an Activist

Movements of people have helped humanity survive and progress over our shared history. Justice-oriented citizens, organized together, have spoken truth to power, often advocating for positions that are initially unpopular with the majorities of people but often later widely supported by that same populace. In fact, over the past century, the most important defenders of democracy have been mobilized movements of everyday people (Dahlum et al., 2019; Davis, 2011, 2016). As Moyer and colleagues (2001) argued, social movements have long offered road maps for citizenship and social change, and activism should be the main lens through which we read history. This view aligns with numerous arguments that claim the purpose of history education, and why we must understand the past, is to foster informed citizens who will make the world better (Barton & Levstik, 2004; Epstein, 2009; Lévesque, 2008; Stearns, 1998; VanSledright, 2011; Wineburg, 2001, 2018). As such, in this book, we argue that history education must teach students and citizens to think like activists as they study the past.

Problematically, most Americans (and especially White Americans) view history through the lens of the important individual. They often credit major historical changes to one person (or a small group). Epstein (2009) and Cuban (2016) have attributed this to a persistent heritage/nationalist approach to history teaching in our schools, where the history classroom is focused on the memorization of names, dates, and places as a form of national celebration. We see this in surveys of the American public about historical events and figures. For example, a majority of Americans believe Abraham Lincoln's Emancipation Proclamation ended slavery (Washington Post & Social Science Research Solutions, 2019), rather than it being the result of decades of abolitionist activism and the passage of the 13th Amendment (which was also not the result of one person's actions). Americans credit much of the successes of the civil rights movement to one individual, Martin Luther King Jr. (CBS News, 2013), with support from Rosa Parks, rather than the larger movement of civil rights activists who had worked for decades after the Civil War for racial justice. While this is an ahistorical view of the past (as there are few, maybe no, examples from history where one person made a significant social change alone), it is likely the result of a long tradition of American students learning history mainly through the stories of important individuals.

At the same time, Americans generally have a negative view of activists and movements, despite their importance in improving society. In fact, a majority of Americans do not perceive key movements of the past and present as making the United States better; this includes the labor, anti–Vietnam War, LGBTQ rights, Occupy Wall Street, Black Lives Matter, and #MeToo movements. Only the civil rights movement is viewed positively by a majority of Americans (Ipsos, 2019). We speculate that a lack of history instruction around the role that activists and movements have played in the past, in conjunction with an abundance of history classroom materials, textbooks, and popular media that glorify the achievements of individual leaders, has contributed to this perception among the general public. As VanSledright (2006) has argued, many students dislike school history because it presents the past as a fait accompli, or settled matter, involving no interpretation or debate (which is the opposite of how historians view it). Cuban (2016) has argued that the longstanding tradition of the heritage/nationalist approach to history education and its emphasis on the "great leaders" have contributed to American students' dislike of the discipline.

For most young people, it is not engaging nor, frankly, useful to learn about powerful individuals from a history that is far removed from their world or lived experiences. If students (and citizens) see history only shaped by famous individuals, then they may see no reason for learning about it. Moreover, this approach to the study of history is particularly unappealing to students of color and students from other nondominant groups, as it does not align with their lived experiences and those of their families' histories. As Epstein (2009) argued, Americans of color (and we would add women, immigrants, the poor and working classes, and queer people) situate their histories within a collective model for changing society; as a result, they should be rightfully suspicious of a history curriculum that is overly focused on the achievements of famous individuals.

Additionally, we argue that the heritage/nationalist approach to history education has fostered a general lack of trust in movements by citizens. As Epstein (2009) has argued, a heritage/nationalist approach to history education leads people to seek individuals, rather than groups, as models for changing society. This type of history education sends the message that the people should not collectively try to change society, and especially not participate in organizing and movement building. Instead, the heritage approach sends a message to citizens that we should trust important individuals, rather than the people collectively organized. Then it also makes sense that Americans simply hope for the next elected leader to "come and save them," or perhaps it would be a leader not chosen by the people, as we see a rise in support for authoritarianism in the United States and worldwide (Drutman et al., 2018; Foa & Mounk, 2016; Levitsky & Ziblatt, 2018).

In many ways, we see indicators of this in recent campaigns and elections. We could look at the election of either Barack Obama or Donald Trump. Both candidates argued for social changes (granted that they do so with two very different visions of social change), which inspired voters (granted that they are two very different groups of voters) to trust that a single individual could enact their desired social changes. When those leaders are unable to deliver on many of the promised social changes, ultimately the citizens continue to have weakened trust in democracy (as we are seeing with the aforementioned rising support of authoritarianism), or the citizens support their leader disregarding laws or other democratic traditions to achieve their political goals, as some polls suggest (Cox & Jones, 2016). The teaching of history through a heritage/nationalist approach might be one of the factors contributing to the decline of trust and participation in democracy by students and citizens.

Most of the important social changes across history have occurred as a result of activists organized within movements. Therefore, students (and citizens) must be better educated about movements, and they should use an activist lens when examining historical events. Otherwise, citizens will continue to believe that important individuals are the only ones who can make change. This not only leads to a general misunderstanding of historical social change, but also ultimately reduces the number of citizens who are willing to participate in movements for democracy and justice. Instead of asking about the contributions of certain individuals, when examining events in the past, students should ask: "How was change made collectively by the people?" and "What levers of influence were employed to enact that change?" For example, we can see how movements of people reacted to Hurricane Katrina or the Iraq War (rather than how George W. Bush made decisions about them). We can look at runaway people during slavery as individuals trying to escape a life-threatening situation, or we can view them as a movement of resisters trying to stop slavery. We should use this method to look at modern history, such as the women's rights movement or the labor movement, and also for ancient history, such as the Roman slave revolts (73–71 BCE), the First Jewish Revolt (66–70 CE), or the movement of women seeking equality with men in Heian Japan (794–1185 CE). While it is true that the ancient historical record is more incomplete than the modern historical record, we as educators (with the help of historians and anthropologists) must dig deeper to find those sources and examples that can help students understand movements working for justice.

By helping students learn about past movements of people working toward social change, the students are able to understand that one important utility of history is to help inform the present. It offers students an understanding of how power was created and maintained, as well as how people, especially from oppressed groups, worked to change society. It also teaches that history is unfinished business, where historians and citizens are continually examining and reexamining evidence and narratives from the past to inform solutions to present-day problems. As the historian Carl Becker (1932) argued almost 90 years ago, every person is a historian, and "every generation, our own included, will, must inevitably, understand the past and anticipate the future in the light of its own restricted experience" (p. 235). In the end, it is the citizen, seeking a utility for the study of history, who will be responsible for deciding what narratives are most compelling, usually in service of understanding their present world and how it came to be that way, and how the future society might be shaped.

APPROACHES TO HISTORY EDUCATION

Epstein (2009) has argued that there are four main approaches to history teaching: nationalist, disciplinary, participatory democratic, and critical. In her analysis, she found that certain history approaches were able to better help students understand oppression, especially in regard to racism (and we would extend that analysis to other forms of oppression, including sexism, classism, homophobia, and nativism). In this section, we outline the types of "thinking" argued for by the various approaches described by Epstein, and we specifically situate our "thinking like an activist" approach within a critical view of history education.

The nationalist approach, what Cuban (2016) also called the heritage approach, emphasizes cultural assimilation and contends that the purpose of history is to provide a shared national narrative that creates a sense of unity. Advocates of the nationalist approach, seen in the work of Ravitch and Finn (1987), Gagnon (1989), and others, generally praise American diversity, but they argue that "the nation extended freedom and citizenship rights and equality to all and the accomplishments of disenfranchised groups, as well as the nation's steady unfolding of freedom and rights, illustrated the strength of the nation's democratic creed" (Epstein, 2009, p. 13). This approach to history education is essentially arguing that students should be "thinking like a nationalist" when examining the past, where they uncritically accept the premise that the United States is continually addressing inequity, by design or default. It sends the message that the nation has an exceptionalism that should never be questioned. History educators working from a nationalist perspective may problematically teach that social problems have been generally solved in the past and that the United States continues, somewhat easily, on its quest for freedom for all (which will one day soon be realized). While they may be partially correct that racism, sexism, classism, homophobia, and nativism have decreased in some ways (the United States now allows women to vote, has laws against many forms of de jure racial segregation, and no longer commits gays and lesbians to mental institutions or prisons because of their sexual orientation), there is little evidence that social inequity and oppression have significantly declined; they may simply appear more invisible or function differently today. Instead, there is growing evidence that segregation and inequity have become worse over the past three decades (Kochhar & Cilluffo, 2018; Semega et al., 2019). As such, the nationalist/heritage approach to history education deters students from critically evaluating or interpreting the past, as it presents a singular narrative from the perspective of dominant groups in society (to be learned and remembered for unity purposes).

The disciplinary approach focuses on the thinking skills of professional historians with the goal of promoting "in the young the epistemological orientation and skills of professional historians" (Epstein, 2009, p. 13). These educators promote the acquisition of conceptual categories (historical significance, empathy, causes, and consequences) and procedural knowledge (analysis and evaluation of primary and secondary sources) that historians use in their work. They make clear that the purpose of history is to avoid using "contemporary ways of thinking and behaving to past people and events" (p. 13). This perspective views history primarily in a disciplinary sense, rather than as a subject, to prepare students for democratic life (granted, it still may help serve that goal).

The participatory democratic approach positions history as a device for active civic participation in democratic societies. The approach "encourages young people to recognize the multifaceted nature of social issues and draw upon a wide range of knowledge to solve contemporary problems" (Epstein, 2009, p. 14). It promotes citizenship education as the ultimate goal of the history classroom and asks students to consider how events in the past served or did not serve the common good. This approach views history as preparation for democratic life, rather than as a means to reconstruct society (granted, it still may help serve that goal).

The critical approach stresses that history must help students and citizens create a more just society. This approach is a "means to enable young people to develop skills that disrupt oppressive hierarchies and work toward more equitable societies" (Epstein, 2009, p. 14). It promotes examining history through racial, gender, class, and sexual orientation lenses, and it highlights the role that economic and political structures have played in producing oppression. This approach views history as a vehicle to teach students how the current social structures came to be and how we can use the past to inform the ways we can make the world fairer in the present and future.

TYPES OF THINKING IN HISTORY

Thinking Like a Historian Approach

Much of the reforms in history education over the past three decades have been from a cognitive perspective, or what Epstein (2009) labeled the disciplinary approach. With a foundation in the work of Sam Wineburg (1991a, 1991b, 2001) and other cognitive psychologists, numerous scholars have argued that history education should be modeled after the thinking processes of academic historians (Baron, 2012, 2013; Martin & Monte-Sano, 2008; Monte-Sano, 2008, 2010, 2016; Reisman, 2012a, 2012b; Reisman & Wineburg, 2008; Yeager & Wilson, 1997). Rooted in the work of Jean Piaget (1950/2001, 1970) and Jerome Bruner (1960), this work focuses on the individual and their cognitive processes. This approach to history education has been dubbed by some as "thinking like a historian."

According to Wineburg (1991a), historians think about the past through three main processes:

> (a) corroboration, the act of comparing documents with one another; (b) sourcing, the act of looking first to the source of the document before reading the body of the text; and (c) contextualization, the act of situating a document in a concrete temporal and spatial context. (p. 77)

Students should use these processes and should engage in a close reading of historical sources, considering what documents say and the language that their creators used to say it. Ultimately, these thinking processes should become habits of the mind used by students and adults to interpret the past.

This stance focuses the study of history on individual cognitive processes and prepares students to use the same modes that historians use to analyze the past. While this is an important skill for students to develop, this approach does not inherently prepare them to be agents of change or to consider ways that the study of history informs social action. Thinking like a historian can serve as a tool for understanding inequity (and many teachers do employ it in critical ways), but it can also be used in ways where students' questions are asked within traditional historical frameworks or without questioning dominant narratives of history.

Thinking Like a Democratic Citizen Approach

More recently, another group of scholars has argued that an overemphasis on individual thinking processes neglects the social uses of history as a tool for democratic citizenship and the common good. Epstein (2009) labeled this group as representing the democratic participatory approach to history education. Rooted in sociocultural theory and the work of Vygotsky (1978) and Wertsch (1998, 2002), and with a foundation in the work of Levstik and Barton (2001) and others, these scholars make the case that history is a social practice, and, in particular, it can have a positive impact on the development of democratic citizens (Lévesque, 2008; Levy et al., 2013; Martell, 2013, 2020). For instance, Barton (2002) has challenged the work of cognitive psychologists in history education, such as Wineburg, as "ignor[ing] factors that extend beyond individual psychology, such as cultural norms, economic structures, societal institutions, or the environment" (p. 272).

This approach to history education has been dubbed by some as "thinking like a citizen," or more accurately as "thinking like a democratic citizen."

Within this approach, the study of history is as much about the past as it is about the present. Barton and Levstik (2004) argued that there are four specific actions that history students should be expected to perform: identify, analyze, respond morally, and display. When students take an identification stance, they embrace connections between themselves and people and events of the past. When they take the analytical stance, they establish causal linkages in history by connecting the past to the present. When they take the moral response stance, they are asked to remember, admire, and condemn people and events in the past. When they take the exhibition stance, they display and exhibit information about the past. Ultimately, these stances become the cultural tools used by citizens to understand the past and how it is connected to the present.

The democratic citizenship approach focuses the study of history on sociocultural processes and prepares students to think about the past in the ways that citizens should. While this is an important skill for students to develop, this approach does not inherently prepare them to be agents of change or consider ways that history informs social action. Similar to thinking like a historian, thinking like a democratic citizen can serve as a tool for understanding inequity (and again, many teachers do employ it in critical ways), but it can also be used in ways where students' questions are asked within traditional historical frameworks or without questioning dominant narratives of history.

Thinking Like an Activist Approach

Working from critical theory (Freire, 1974; Freire & Macedo, 2005; Magill & Salinas, 2019), we argue that "thinking like an activist" is an essential third approach in history education (see Figure 2.1 for a comparison of the three perspectives of history education). This approach to history is aligned with what Epstein (2009) labeled critical perspectives on teaching history. If we want to change the world for the better, history teachers must help students understand how they can think like a historian, a democratic citizen, *and* an activist. At its core, this approach involves helping them think about how the past was changed by collective movements of people. One of the main flaws of traditional historical study is that it leaves students with an impression that important individuals were the main drivers of the past. Historians often organize the past around eras of kings or presidents, and even when discussing social movements, progress is often attributed to important leaders (e.g., Susan B. Anthony, Martin Luther King Jr., César Chávez). Yet, as Howard Zinn (2002, September 18) argued, movement leaders are only the figureheads allowed to represent the larger masses of people. With that perspective, it is also important to analyze if those leaders ever strayed from their

Figure 2.1. Comparing History Education Approaches

Thinking Like a Historian	Thinking Like a Democratic Citizen	Thinking Like an Activist
Origin: cognitive psychology; thinking processes of professional historians	Origin: sociocultural theory; tools citizens need to analyze history relevant to their participation in democracy	Origin: critical theory; the historical ideas and actions needed for building movements and achieving justice
Core components (Wineburg, 1991a, p. 77): (a) corroboration, the act of comparing documents with one another; (b) sourcing, the act of looking first to the source of the document before reading the body of the text; (c) contextualization, the act of situating a document in a concrete temporal and spatial context.	Core components (Barton & Levstik, 2004, pp. 7–10): (a) identify, embrace connections between themselves and people and events of the past; (b) analyze, establish causal linkages in history; (c) respond morally, asked to remember, admire, and condemn people and events in the past; (d) display, exhibit information about the past.	Core components: (a) cultural preparation, creating a new vision of what society can be instead of the status quo; it involves unlearning oppressive structures and building solidarity; (b) critical analysis, developing the ability to recognize how oppression is constructed and power structures are replicated; (c) collective action, which involves organization building, confrontation, and noncooperation.

movement's ultimate goals (which can sometimes happen when they begin to develop relationships and gain favor with people in positions of power).

Related to this idea is that the narratives that people use to make sense of the past are framed by their social structures. As James Wertsch (2002, 2008a, 2008b, 2012) has found, communities use certain narrative templates to interpret the past and to develop their collective memory. He wrote,

> Narrative templates are generalized schematic structures that do not include such concrete information. They are cookie cutter plots or storylines that can be used to generate multiple specific narratives . . . [they are] used repeatedly by a mnemonic community to interpret multiple specific events by fitting them into a schematic plot line. (Wertsch, 2012, p. 175)

Numerous scholars have highlighted that the freedom-quest narrative template is the most commonly used template to understand the past among students (and the general public) in the United States (Barton & Levstik, 2004; Hawkman & Castro, 2017; Lévesque, 2008; Oto, 2020; VanSledright, 2008; VanSledright & Afflerbach, 2000; Wertsch & O'Connor, 1994). This narrative template presents a major problem for history being used as a device for social change, as it gives citizens a false sense that history (at least in the United States) is one of continual progress and improvement. This template often disregards the many moments when society regresses, and it implies that if citizens do nothing, society will continue to get better. It also implies that racism is rare in the United States (Oto, 2020). As such, it is important to help students better understand how historical narratives are constructed and, more importantly, used to justify the status quo, which maintains systems of inequity. We need to leverage previous work on history education and center the classroom on how inequity developed over time and how by understanding the past we can create a more just and equitable future.

The most important changes in human history were driven by movements of people working for justice, rather than by important individuals. Instead, important individuals have only been able to contribute to changing a society when pressured by the masses. If we are to have students "do history," they must examine movements of change as the main focus of their historical analysis. If we have students look at historical examples, they should inquire how collective activists changed the system.

This is not an idea outside the mainstream of historical study. Over the past 3 decades, there has been an important shift in the academic historian community. Numerous historians have emerged, focusing their work on justice and equity. We have seen a blooming of historians examining social history; some of the most notable historians and historical works of our lifetime have captured underrepresented voices and have asked questions about how unfairness was built into our current society. This includes such notable academic histories as Laurel Thatcher Ulrich's (1990) *A Midwife's Tale*, Ibram X. Kendi's (2017) *Stamped from the Beginning*, Eric Foner's (1990/2017) *A Short History of Reconstruction*, Peter Frankopan's (2015) *The Silk Roads*, and Tamim Ansary's (2009) *Destiny Disrupted*. These historians centered inequity in their analysis of the past to help us better understand our present. While some academic historians criticize his work, another prime example is Howard Zinn's (1980/2003) *A People's History of the United States*, which focuses on the long history of injustice in the United States and is probably the most widely read historical work of the past half-century.

USING ACTIVIST THEORIES TO UNDERSTAND HISTORY

Based on this concept that the purpose of history is to understand social change in the past and how it applies to the present, we posit that the study of history should be framed around justice and that the vehicle for achieving justice is social activism. As Cynthia Tyson (2003) has argued, we must add social activism to the knowledge, skills, and values of social studies education, and this book outlines how that can be applied specifically within the discipline of history. To accomplish this, we look to the theories of social activists Bill Moyer, JoAnn MacAllister, Mary Lou Finley, and Steven Soifer (2001) and George Lakey (2004).

A Manual for Direct Action

At the height of the civil rights movement, and based on their work within that movement, Oppenheimer and Lakey (1965) developed *A Manual for Direct Action*, which outlined how to build a justice movement. Building on that work, Lakey (2004) and Lakey and colleagues (2016) later created "Strategies for Living a Revolution," which included the five overlapping and fluid stages of a social movement: cultural preparation, organization building, confrontation, mass political and economic noncooperation, and parallel institutions. To illustrate how this model functions, they used numerous historical examples, including the Indian independence movement, student sit-ins during the civil rights movement, and the Otpor movement in Serbia. He highlighted that successful movements always take time and involve concerted effort.

Cultural preparation. Lakey (2004) argued that cultural preparation is politicization or consciousness-raising. To build a new culture, as a group people need to envision something different from the current world governed by power hierarchies. This is when groups start to form into movements and begin to build a culture of resistance; it is the place to unlearn racism, sexism, and religious bigotry. A society cannot be rebuilt on old power structures, and the first step in the process is to recognize and acknowledge those structures that oppress. For example, it was Black activists in the South who during Reconstruction (and before) began to envision a new society based on racial justice. These groups of activists laid the intellectual, legal, and political groundwork for what would become the modern civil rights movement.

Organization building. Once a movement forms around a shared vision for the future, organization building is the key second step (Lakey, 2004). Spontaneous movements rarely last, nor do they result in systematic change. This is a stage when movements often fail. Radical activists often find it difficult to organize. Any successful movement must be "both visionary and get the job done" (p. 141). Lakey provided the Student Nonviolent Coordinating Committee as a prime example of successful organization building. In 1963–1964, this group of students, facing enormous danger, created an extensive network of freedom houses and freedom schools to organize and push back on the deeply racist social system in Mississippi. Eventually, this organization would win important allies, especially on the national level, that began to lead to social change, albeit slowly.

Confrontation. Confrontation is a large and prolonged drama. In this stage, the activists in the movement must establish themselves as the "good guys" and the opposition as the "bad guys" (Lakey, 2004). This includes public conflict aimed at weakening support for the opposition, who maintain the status quo. Small and countless protests are better than a few larger ones (although larger ones can occur to raise awareness, it is the smaller ones that show those in power that the movement is serious). Again, looking to the civil rights movement, the numerous campaigns of sit-ins at lunch counters and bus stations are a prime example of this type of confrontation; eventually, those actions forced the federal government to react. The power holders must be continually put in a dilemma. If they serve the protesters, "racism took a hit. If they were either attacked by civilians or arrested, racism also took a hit" (p. 146). However, this is when many movements have "lost the game," as they are unable to sustain smaller and targeted protests or to contrast their behavior with that of the oppressors.

Mass political and economic noncooperation. During this stage, the movement needs to grow (Lakey, 2004). To do this, there must be massive noncooperation, which also begins to win over the public. Without public support (which often initially opposed the movement for change), the movement is unlikely to make any systematic change to society. For example, seeing civil rights protesters, sometimes children, attacked with water hoses and police dogs helped make the cause for desegregation a wider American cause. Boycotts were used and various other tactics helped nonactivists join in the struggle. It should also be noted that many movements have often failed at this stage. Those with power can simply wait it out and allow a return to the status quo. In the case of the civil rights movement, the activists' advocating for sustained noncooperation eventually made it impossible for the public to continue to side with state governments and police forces defending the status quo; they could no longer wait it out, and it forced the federal government to take action through legislation and enforcement.

Parallel institutions. The final goal is to create parallel institutions that can take the place of oppressive social structures. These institutions are "sprung from the seeds of the organizing stage" (Lakey, 2004, p. 153) and "become part of the infrastructure of the new society . . . this strategic model proposes a bottom-up restructuring" (p. 154). The new society is "co-created with mainstream people who have realized that the old way is no longer tenable" (p. 154). The new view of the general public is aligned with the activists' vision. While it may not mean that all is solved, all future decisions begin with the baseline established with the movement (rather than the previous status quo). For instance, by the 1970s, new institutions were created within government to ensure equal access to all and the desegregation of communities. Granted, by the 1980s, many of those institutions began to be targeted by groups that wanted to return to the previous society (and in many ways these groups continue to seek this). Movements must continue to push for social change and realize that oppressive forces will continue to find ways to take back power from the people.

Movement Action Plan

Paralleling some of the ideas of Lakey (2004) and Lakey and colleagues (2016), and based on their involvement in the civil rights and anti-war movements, Moyer and colleagues (2001) created their "Movement Action Plan" (MAP). MAP described a series of eight stages that social movements use to influence progress and to achieve positive social change: (1) status quo, (2) normal channels fail, (3) conditions ripen, (4) take off, (5) perception of failure, (6) win public support, (7) success, and (8) continuation. These eight stages are grouped into four periods: steady state (stage 1), buildup of stress in the system (stages 2–4), seen as a general problem (stages 5–6), and resolution (stages 7–8). Moyer and colleagues use the antinuclear movement that started in the late 1940s as a key movement to illustrate each of the eight stages. They highlight that many movements are able to launch (take off) but are often unable to sustain their momentum once they begin to perceive failure.

Steady state and buildup of stress in the system. Moyer and colleagues (2001) contended that the steady state begins with normal times, when the people do not generally recognize problems exist (status quo). Social problems are sustained by systems that make them almost invisible to most. Small groups of activists recognize the problems and form local opposition groups advocating for change; they tend to use established channels, which often prove that they do not work (normal channels fail), and the activists begin to research potential solutions to the problems. Next, the public begins to have some awareness (conditions ripen), and the activists begin to gain some support with the general public, but usually not a critical mass. Next, there is usually a trigger event that "starkly reveals to the general public for the first time that a serious problem exists" (p. 54). A historical example from the civil rights struggle might include Rosa Parks's protest of the Montgomery, Alabama, bus system or the police attack on peaceful protesters at the Pettus Bridge in Selma, Alabama. The event instills a large amount of moral outrage. The new social movement rapidly gains attention, and it now has a larger spotlight (takeoff).

Seen as a general problem. Moyer and colleagues (2001) argued that there is a general increase in hopelessness and despair on the part of the activists (perception of failure); the movement's participants begin to see that things are not changing, and there is a decline in participation. This is when many movements fail, as they are unable to overcome this challenge and cannot sustain their cause over the long term. At this time, there is often an emergence of rebel groups that present potentially fatal problems within the movement. To overcome this, movements must stay committed to their original values and vision. The rebels within the movement may even make the rest of the movement appear more mainstream and acceptable to the general public (win public support). At this point, movements must make a public case for the social change they desire and seek a majority of support. They must show how the majority of the people are impacted by the problem. This puts the problem on the political agenda, and movements force those in positions of power to acknowledge the problem, while also proposing possible alternatives.

Resolution. Activists must know that there is never an ending to their movement, and "there is only the continual cycle of social movements and their sub-issues and sub-movements" (Moyer et al., 2001, p. 85). In the resolution stage, a large majority begins to oppose the status quo, and many power holders split off and change positions (success). Power holders are forced to change policies (granted this stage can take substantial time, as power holders attempt to make minimal reforms or delay implementation in hopes that the previous status quo may return). Finally, there is extended success and a paradigm shift within the society. Yet the struggle continues with a focus on sub-issues and mobilization to prevent any attempts at backlash, as those who lose power will demand a return to previous times (continuation).

Interpreting History Through Activist Lenses

While Lakey's (2004) and Moyer and colleagues' (2001) theories offer slightly different descriptions of the stages of successful movements, there is considerable overlap between the two. The four periods that Moyer and colleagues organize their MAP around have significant parallelism to Lakey's stages. As such, we argue that these theories offer several important ideas that students can use to analyze the past and consider how change was successfully or unsuccessfully enacted. To create a workable framework that students can use to analyze movements in history, we have derived our framework from these two theories.

We argue that the "thinking like an activist" framework is comprised of three main components that successful movements for social change have included: (1) cultural preparation, (2) critical analysis, and (3) collective action.

By analyzing past events through these components, students will not only gain a better understanding of how social change occurred in the past, but also be better equipped to be a part of social change in the present and future.

Cultural preparation involves creating a new vision of what society can be instead of the status quo; it involves unlearning oppressive structures and building solidarity. Lakey (2004) has described cultural preparation as the need for activists to build a culture of resistance and envision a new society. He argued that before movements can engage in social change, their collective activists must unlearn the internalized messages that they receive from the society around them.

To use the concept of cultural preparation to analyze the past, students would first have to understand what the status quo was at a particular time. Teachers can provide students with primary sources from the movement and from those who opposed the movement, and they can also provide sources that illuminate the prevailing thinking of the time that offers contrast. Next, students must describe what the world was like prior to the movement and what the movement envisioned that the world should look like in the future. Finally, students identify the methods that were used by the movement and determine if it was successful in influencing change (at the time or in the future).

Critical analysis, which involves developing sociopolitical consciousness, is the ability to recognize how oppression is constructed and how power structures are replicated. Moyer and colleagues (2001) described political analysis as a key component of MAP. Without understanding and documenting the problem that exists or the structures that govern particular problems, it is difficult to organize an effective movement. To use this concept to analyze the past, students should look for the political, economic, and social structures in place that perpetuate a particular problem. For instance, if they were analyzing civil rights in the mid-20th century, they might list the history of racial slavery, Jim Crow laws, discrimination in employment and education, and the lack of voting rights as structural problems that allowed segregation to continue. They should be able to take various types of oppression and analyze how they affected African Americans at the time, as well as analyze how those historical issues persist today and contribute to current inequity. This is where the teacher should consider providing secondary sources that may be particularly helpful, as the work of historians (anthropologists, political scientists, and other social scientists) may be able to provide important frames or context.

Collective action is the work of activists; it is how movements enact change. Lakey (2004) described this as including organization building, or the ability to grow support among the general public, and the use of confrontation and noncooperation to weaken power holders' control by applying pressure. To use this concept to analyze the past, students should consider a movement's various actions. Rarely do movements use only one lever to enact change; instead, they use multiple social actions at once to build solidarity, gain public support, and engage in protest and civil disobedience. For example, when examining the modern civil rights movement, students should be able to recognize that civil rights activists organized and participated in mass rallies, used the court system by filing lawsuits, engaged in civil disobedience (such as sit-ins and prohibited marches), and worked behind the scenes to convince politicians to vote for proposed legislation. By using all of these types of action, the movement was more successful.

THINKING LIKE AN ACTIVIST CLASSROOM TOOL

This "thinking like an activist" framework is the basis for a tool that we suggest students use to analyze historical events to determine if they involved successful movements for change (and it provides a model for building future movements for change). Students should use the following three components to analyze events in the past (or present). We suggest using the associated questions to help them examine the actions of activists in movements:

- Cultural preparation: Did a group of people at the time want to change society, and did they have a vision for how it might look different? If so, what was that vision and how was it different?
- Critical analysis: Did a group of people at the time outline and help educate the public about a particular type of oppression and the ways that they could work against it? Did they make the case to the public that alternatives to the status quo would benefit all?
- Collective action: Did a group of people at the time engage in collective actions? (Was there a "trigger event" that gained public attention? What methods were used to raise public awareness?) Did the movement gain public support? Did the group's collective actions lead to a change in society? Is there still a legacy of this today?

We do not suggest that these are the only questions that should be asked or that all of these questions should be used during every lesson. Rather, we think these questions offer an important starting point to get students to think about history through the work of activists, through the movements that they form, and to center social change on collective action, rather than the lens of the important individual.

We can again use the civil rights movement to illustrate how this tool can be used. Let's imagine that we had students analyze one part of the civil rights movement—the actions of the Southern Christian Leadership Conference after the Montgomery bus boycott. Figure 2.2 provides an example of how one student may evaluate the movement. Notice that the questions intentionally ask the students to focus on the actions of the

Figure 2.2. Thinking Like an Activist Questions

Component	Questions	Potential Student Examples
Cultural preparation: creating a new vision of what society can be instead of the status quo; it involves unlearning oppressive structures and building solidarity.	Did a group of people at the time want to change society, and did they have a vision for how it might look different? If so, what was that vision and how was it different?	Numerous civil rights activists in the South envisioned a society built on integration, including the Southern Christian Leadership Conference (SCLC), Congress of Racial Equality (CORE), and the National Association for the Advancement of Colored People (NAACP).
Critical analysis: developing the ability to recognize how oppression is constructed and how power structures are replicated.	Did a group of people at the time outline and help educate the public about a particular type of oppression and the ways that they could work against it? Did they make the case to the public that alternatives to the status quo would benefit all?	The SCLC, CORE, and NAACP would stage a series of campaigns to educate the public on the issues of racial injustice and would organize mass acts of nonviolence, exposing the racism embedded in society. The reactions of those with power, often using violence on the protesters, illuminated the problem for the public.
Collective action: involves organization building, confrontation, and noncooperation.	Did a group of people at the time engage in collective actions? (Was there a "trigger event" that gained public attention? What methods were used to raise public awareness?) Did the movement gain support? Did the group's collective actions lead to a change in society? Is there still a legacy of this today?	The Rosa Parks bus protest and the following Montgomery bus boycott became a trigger event to raise awareness of the issue. While slow to gain public support at first, over time it grew and became a catalyst for later civil rights legislation and court rulings. Other groups, like the Nation of Islam, Organization of Afro-American Unity, and Black Panther Party offered additional perspectives and activism. Yet the United States still has structural racism and widespread racial inequity, which Black Lives Matter and other groups continue to work against.

group, as opposed to the actions of one leader (or a few leaders). This helps them consider the choices that movements make to create a new vision, to recognize ways to educate the public about the oppressive systems, and to build organizations and change public opinion, which can ultimately lead to social change.

CHAPTER 3

Social Inquiry

Inquiry is how humans understand the world around them. People ask questions and seek evidence to satisfy their curiosities or deepen their understandings. Yet schooling has traditionally not focused on inquiry. Rather, education has been seen as a transmission of information from teacher to student (Richardson, 1997), or what Freire (1970/2000) described as the banking method (where, using the analogy of a bank, the teacher is seen as a depositor of knowledge in the students). However, based on decades of research on teaching and learning, there has been a growing movement of educators advocating for inquiry-based instruction within and across school subject areas (Barron & Darling-Hammond, 2008; Colburn, 2000; Levy et al., 2013). While the definitions of inquiry vary across disciplines, they generally share some commonalities, including the formation of questions (which can be driven by the teacher or the students), the use of disciplinary practices, and the analysis of evidence.

Not all historical inquiries are equal. Linking to the work of Freire (1970/2000), inquiries should be rooted in problem-posing and should be relevant to the lives of the students engaged in them. Students must investigate the past in relation to themselves in the current world (and in a way where the student-teacher learning is reciprocal, and the teacher is not considered the sole authority). The students should see themselves and their ancestors in their inquiries. As Freire (1970/2000) wrote,

> Education as the practice of freedom—as opposed to education as the practice of domination—denies that man is abstract, isolated, independent, and unattached to the world; it also denies that the world exists as a reality apart from people. Authentic reflection considers neither abstract man nor the world without people, but people in their relations with the world. (p. 81)

With this concept in mind, inquiries may be teacher-driven, but students must be able to pose and explore their own questions based on their worldviews, cultural backgrounds, and civic needs.

Within history education, inquiries focus on asking questions about the past, examining evidence (often in the form of primary, secondary, or tertiary sources), and forming historical arguments or narratives. We prefer to use Barton and Levstik's (2004) broad definition of historical inquiry as a process involving "asking questions, gathering and evaluating relevant evidence, and reaching conclusions based on that evidence" (p. 188), as it applies not only to the work of historians, but also to that of citizens (and we would add activists organized in movements). This definition of inquiry is predicated on students using evidence to support their claims regardless of the type of classroom activities that the teacher employs. Whether a teacher uses mock trials, debates, or more traditional source work, the students will be asked to use historical evidence and to consider alterative interpretations or explanations in forming their arguments or stances.

MAKING INQUIRIES SOCIAL

In Chapter 1, we suggested that the word *social* needs to accompany inquiry when we use it in the history classroom, as it spotlights for teachers and students the importance of asking questions and gathering and evaluating evidence through the lens of power relationships in the past (similar to what others have labeled critical inquiries). The goal is to understand the welfare of human beings in a society over time and how equity has or has not been present in those societies. This helps students understand how the past led to the current present and how it will influence the future. It includes not only the human world, but also how humans have impacted the natural world (and how impacts on the natural world may disproportionately impact certain social groups).

If inquiry is to be a tool for justice, it must specifically engage in social inquiries. As Cinthia Salinas and Brooke Blevins (2014) have argued, it is important that historical inquiries challenge students to critically examine the past or look at the role that social identity, power, and privilege have played in history. By intentionally focusing their study of history on equity, students are able to understand how our current society came to be, or how it can be possibly repaired. Often, students learn history through the dominant perspective of the past (even when inquiring about it), and they are part of the transmission (through the official curriculum) of those dominant perspectives over time. To fill this gap, Salinas and Blevins proposed a critical historical inquiry, where students begin to "understand, disrupt and challenge the official curriculum and explore new and diverse perspectives that recognize and honor the unique experiences of linguistically and culturally diverse communities" (p. 38).

Numerous other scholars have pushed different aspects of history education in this same direction in regard to curriculum and teaching (Busey, 2014; Busey & Cruz, 2015; Chandler, 2015; Chandler & McKnight, 2009;

Epstein, 2009; Epstein & Gist, 2015; Epstein et al., 2011; King, 2016; King & Brown, 2014; Rodríguez, 2018; Santiago, 2017, 2019; Woodson, 2015, 2017). Based on this work, we argue that we need to better ensure that history education focuses on equity. While history education should help students understand the nature of the discipline (thinking like a historian) and develop as democratic decisionmakers (thinking like a democratic citizen), it must also serve the important purpose of making the nation and world more just. As such, when students "do history," it is essential that their inquiries focus on social identity and power relationships, as those elements are at the core of how movements were able to create social change over time.

INQUIRIES THROUGH A HISTORICAL THINKING LENS

Over the past 50 years, a series of studies from the field of cognitive psychology has influenced how the discipline of history is taught at the K–12 level. Building on the work of Bruner (1960, 1970), Wineburg (1991a, 1991b, 2001) argued that students engage in historical inquiries that model the thinking processes of academic historians. Unlike the general public, Wineburg (1991a) found that historians rely on several key heuristics, including:

> (a) corroboration, the act of comparing documents with one another; (b) sourcing, the act of looking first to the source of the document before reading the body of the text; and (c) contextualization, the act of situating a document in a concrete temporal and spatial context. (p. 77)

As a result of this work, there has been a blooming of professional development and online resources (e.g., Stanford History Education Group) based on the idea that students should practice interpreting the past using the thinking modes of historians.

Without a doubt, understanding the nature of the discipline and how historians construct the past are incredibly important skills. They are particularly helpful in preparing students for the type of thinking needed to one day become historians. As Carl Becker (1932) argued, every person can be their own historian. They have the capabilities of historical imagination and can use evidence from the historical record to better develop their understanding of the past. In this spirit, developing historical thinking skills helps not only future academic historians, but also citizens as they think about the past. Wineburg (2016, 2018) and Wineburg and Reisman (2015) take this a step further by arguing that the skills of interpretation that historians use can be employed by citizens in their analysis of information in the media and elsewhere.

INQUIRIES THROUGH A DEMOCRATIC CITIZENSHIP LENS

About 20 years ago, a critique of cognitive psychology–oriented views of historical thinking emerged. Building on the sociocultural work of Wertsch (1998), Barton and Levstik (1996, 2003, 2004) contended that historical inquiries should involve the thought processes of democratic citizens. In their view, rooted in what Dewey (1910/1997) called a "felt difficulty," inquiries should involve investigating a problem. Unlike some of the work done by cognitive psychologists, Levstik and Barton (2011) argued that the basic tenets of inquiry are universal across fields. They argued that students' historical thinking should not be modeled after the structures that historians use in their investigations, as it may be too narrow of a skill. Instead, they described historical inquiry broadly as "asking questions, gathering and evaluating relevant evidence, and reaching conclusions based on that evidence" (p. 188). They described the most important component of inquiry as "the connection between evidence and accounts" (p. 198) and that the questions asked should have significance for the cultural and political aspects of society, which they describe as questions that lead to answers that matter. As such, Levstik and Barton (2011) described disciplined inquiry as including the following components: (a) asking questions that are of relevance to the lives of students and their lives as citizens in a democracy; (b) finding information, which can include primary and secondary sources; (c) drawing conclusions from information, including sources from multiple perspectives; and (d) reflecting on possible solutions to problems of the common good (often rooted in historical events or eras).

These types of historical investigations, Barton and Levstik (2003) argued, may not "guarantee that students will develop into effective citizens of a pluralist, participatory democracy, but it does guarantee they will have taken part in some of its key activities" (p. 360). This broader approach to inquiry better prepares students for the work of citizenship in democratic societies, and what Lévesque (2008) described as the citizen's need to make sense of conflicting views and narratives of history in the present. This group acknowledged that history is controversial, culturally bound, and political; it requires citizens to understand it within the study of present politics.

INQUIRIES THROUGH A JUSTICE LENS

Building on the work of cognitive psychologists and sociocultural theorists, but from a critical perspective (Freire, 1970/2000; Freire & Macedo, 2005; Magill & Salinas, 2019), we argue that historical inquiries must focus explicitly on justice and how movements of people organized for justice. You cannot truly understand the past by primarily examining the acts of individuals. Important individuals have only been able to contribute to a change in society when they were pressured by the masses. Moreover, you cannot understand individual actors in history without an examination of their social identities and how those identities related to power in societies. As we argued in Chapters 1 and 2, all of world history can be organized around movements of people and the collective actions that they took to stop oppression. At the core of this idea is an understanding of how power functions, how it often replicates the status quo (usually benefitting a small group at the expense of everyone else), and how power can possibly be re-distributed to create more equitable societies. Ultimately, historical inquiry must serve the purpose of helping students understand how injustice occurs and how society can be changed to be more just.

While we see value in both the cognitive and sociocultural perspectives of history learning, we argue that a critical element must be embedded in all inquiries. Specifically, for inquiries to be social, they must:

1. Focus on social identities, power, and oppression.
2. Include more authentic voices, especially of nondominant groups.
3. Examine collective action and movement building.

Inquiries, in themselves, do not by default include a focus on these three characteristics. While social inquiries may not always perform all three of these tasks simultaneously, it is crucial that students are regularly engaging in historical investigations with these characteristics in mind, as these characteristics prepare them to think not only like a historian or a democratic citizen, but also like an activist.

Social Identities

Social inquiries focus on social identities and group membership and how they relate to power in societies. Students must routinely consider how different people or groups held (or did not hold) social privilege and how that impacted how they experienced events or issues of the time. Students should have regular opportunities to examine how collective memory is formed, including how dominant groups exercise authority over the mainstream historical narratives and how nondominant groups use counter-narratives (Castro, 2014; King, 2016; Salinas & Blevins, 2014; Salinas et al., 2012; Wertsch, 2000; Wertsch & O'Connor, 1994). It is important for students to gain a deeper understanding of the lived experiences of people of color, women, the poor and working classes, and LGBTQ people and how these experiences relate to social structures that maintain privilege and power for dominant groups.

In practice, this would demand that teachers carefully monitor the historical narratives, collective memories, and narrative templates embedded in the sources that they use in the classroom. Often, especially to teachers from dominant social groups, the embedded perspectives of dominant groups may be invisible. Teachers need to be conscious of the reality that they may be selecting sources that represent the perspectives of people or groups in power. Instead, inquiries must be critical. The history classroom must be a contested space to uncover and confront inconsistencies in the historical record and to reveal voices that were often intentionally silenced or erased from the historical record. Students should be asked to be the interpreters of the past. They should be partners with teachers in asking inquiry questions and finding sources (and deciding on the events to direct their focus).

Authentic Voices

Social inquiries attempt to authentically represent the voices of people who are often missing, misrepresented, or marginalized in the historical record. We find the work of Bishop (1990), from within the field of literacy, particularly helpful. She argued that learning must involve "windows" and "mirrors," where "the history and traditions that are important to any one cultural group [windows] . . . invite comparisons to their own [mirrors]" (p. x). Yet simply adding windows and mirrors is not enough, as it is very possible that underrepresented voices can be added to the curriculum in inauthentic or inaccurate ways. While representation is important, how these voices are represented is more important.

Dominant group-serving narratives. History teachers should avoid presenting narratives that only serve dominant groups. It is not uncommon for history teachers to only present the stories and voices of people of color, women, the poor and working classes, or LGBTQ people when they serve the dominant narrative, which often portrays groups in power as benevolent or not responsible for their actions. As King (2016) has argued, mainstream historical narratives are fraught with racist ideas. Moreover, the history of people of color, and especially African Americans, has often been appropriated to further racist ideas (King & Womac, 2014). Along those lines, history teachers, intentionally or unintentionally, may exclude any narratives that do not serve the dominant ideological views of the past (or present). For example, when teaching the modern civil rights movement, history teachers often sanctify and sanitize the work of modern civil rights movement leaders. For instance, Martin Luther King Jr.'s more radical positions are hidden (e.g., redistribution of wealth and opposition to militarism and the Vietnam War), and teaching civil rights leaders who advocated for a more forceful response to White supremacy (e.g., Malcolm X, the Black Panther Party, more radical members of SNCC) is avoided. Students should not only learn about nondominant groups from the view of the historical, political, geographic, and economic sources from the dominant cultures, but also incorporate those people who are typically marginalized in the curriculum.

Essentializing narratives. History teachers should present narratives that do not essentialize the experiences of nondominant groups. Rather, groups' histories should be presented with complex nuances and should avoid overgeneralization. It is not uncommon for history teachers to stereotype the experiences of people of color, women, the poor and working classes, immigrants, and LGBTQ people. It is much easier to add a woman figure here or a person of color there, rather than center their narratives and those of others in the curriculum, as that involves completely rethinking how the curriculum is taught. It easier to lump all the experiences of people of color into one collective experience. Noddings (2001) has described this as the tradition of "adding women and stir" in the history classroom (or what we describe more broadly as "add diversity and stir").

In contrast, Santiago (2019) outlined an important framework that can help history teachers foster what she labeled anti-essentialist historical inquiries. She argued that,

> (a) the experiences of people of color cannot be essentialized, (b) inquiry can be a useful tool in encouraging historical reasoning that considers such racial/ethnic nuance, and (c) collective memory might be leveraged to encourage students to develop such relational analysis. (p. 114)

Related to this, Santiago and Castro (in press) described anti-essentialist historical inquiry in practice as including the following: learning how historical narratives are constructed, using sources that expose multiple dimensions, engaging with questions that are not easy to answer and cause cognitive dissonance (grapple with two or more contradictory ideas), and applying historical thinking skills critically and crafting an interpretation of past events.

Monolithic narratives. History teachers should present the complexities of nondominant groups, including their diversity in worldviews and cultures. They should avoid monolithic narratives, or what Chimamanda Ngozi Adichie (2009) called the danger of a "single story" (in her talk on conceptions of Africa). This includes presenting nondominant groups as having members (and multiple leaders) with differing and sometimes conflicting perspectives. Typically, dominant social groups are presented with more complexity than nondominant groups. This is especially the case when most historical inquiries tend to include multiple sources from dominant groups' perspectives. It is not uncommon in a typical historical inquiry to see several sources created by straight White men (moreover, it is common for historical inquiries to only include sources created by straight White men). This issue is exacerbated when sources from nondominant groups are included in a tokenized way. For instance, a lesson on immigration from the early 20th century might include one source from Latinx immigrants; while that one source adds diversity (and is a step in the right direction), it presents only one of many Latinx experiences. Migration from the Dominican Republic to New York during this time was very different than migration from Mexico to Texas, for example. Even within the Mexican migration experience, there were differences based on geography, class, and skin color. Yet only including one source may leave students thinking all Latinx experiences were the same. To address this during history lessons, teachers and students should seek sources that present the diverse and sometimes conflicting views from specific nondominant communities. Teachers should consider the differences that exist within communities (in the same way that they should be considering the differences that exist between communities).

Collective Action and Movement Building

Social inquiries help students understand the ways that activists engage in collective action and how movements form. Students should have opportunities to analyze historical events in relation to the three phases of movement building: (1) cultural preparation, (2) critical analysis, and (3) collective action. While these phases are explained in depth in Chapters 1 and 2, they are briefly defined as follows (including questions students should ask):

- Cultural preparation involves creating a new vision of what society can be instead of the status quo; it involves unlearning oppressive structures and building solidarity. Did a group of people at the time want to change society, and did they have a vision for how it might look different? If so, what was that vision and how was it different?
- Critical analysis, or developing sociopolitical consciousness, is the ability to recognize how oppression is constructed and how power structures are replicated. Did a group of people at the time outline and help educate the public about a particular type of oppression and the ways that they could work against it? Did they make the case to the public that alternatives to the status quo would benefit all?
- Collective action is the work of activists; it is how movements enact change. Did a group of people at the time engage in collective actions? (Was there a "trigger event" that gained public attention? What methods were used to raise public awareness?) Did the movement gain support? Did the group's collective actions lead to a change in society?

By using activist frameworks to analyze the past, students are better able to gauge their attempts to change society and apply that understanding to social change in our present times. In combination with investigating the role of social identity and power, plus a more authentic historical representation of groups from the past, it allows students to gain a fuller picture of human history and how it might be a tool for understanding our present (and future) world. Ultimately, this type of social inquiry allows students to imagine how they might (organized with others) build a better society in the future.

CHAPTER 4

Critical Multiculturalism

With Taylor Collins, Framingham Public Schools

In August 2019, to mark the 400th anniversary of the arrival of the first enslaved African people to what became the United States, *The New York Times Magazine* launched the 1619 Project, which was the start of an ongoing project examining the role of slavery in the past and present. Since then, various organizations (such as the Pulitzer Center and the Zinn Education Project) have begun developing the 1619 Project–related resources to help PreK–12 teachers better teach about slavery. In the year after its release, many of our colleagues and friends have asked us about the 1619 Project and if it was changing how teachers taught about slavery. In our recent memory, few media events have put this bright a public spotlight on history education. The only one that comes close may be Lin-Manuel Miranda's award-winning musical *Hamilton*, which was based on the life story of Alexander Hamilton and intentionally cast artists of color in its main roles. For years after its arrival on Broadway, we routinely met people who have found a love for the era of the early U.S. republic after watching the musical or listening to the soundtrack. They also frequently ask if teachers were teaching the "Founding Fathers" differently as a result of it.

Americans' fascination with *Hamilton* is related to their interest in the 1619 Project. Both have brought attention, albeit in very different ways, to the role of race and power in American history. They are essentially public history curricula, teaching the populace about various periods in the past. They have made Americans, many of whom may have detested their school history classes, interested in the history of the nation and curious to learn more. We do not think that this interest stems purely from the thoughtful presentation (or perhaps even advertising) of the 1619 Project or *Hamilton*; rather, we think it is because the American public is incredibly interested in learning about the history of power and oppression in our collective past.

However, these projects have encountered controversy. Both the 1619 Project and *Hamilton* have been critiqued by historians, media personalities, and members of the general public. One important critique of *Hamilton* is that it portrayed Hamilton as having abolitionist views on slavery, which he did not; his views were more nuanced and complicated (Keller, 2018;

Schuessler, 2016). Meanwhile, a small group of historians used their status in the field in an attempt to discredit the 1619 Project's interpretation of history, as it did not align with their views of the American Revolution (Bynum et al., 2019; Serwer, 2019; Wilentz, 2020). This has resulted in a serious discussion about the 1619 Project and how history is used, with some conservative media outlets and politicians (including Donald Trump) using the controversy in an attempt to discredit the project altogether (Linge, 2020). While some may argue that these debates are distracting, we would like to think they are positive and model the exact type of justice-oriented thinking that we hope students will engage in when studying the past.

We also think this is part of the reason why so many Americans dislike school history—it is routinely cited as one of students' least favorite or least interesting subjects in school (Cuban, 1991; Schug et al., 1984; Shaughnessy & Haladyna, 1985; VanSledright, 2008, 2011). As we argued in Chapter 2, school history typically focuses on the memorization of names, dates, and places as a form of national celebration (Cuban, 2016; Epstein, 2009). Instead, we suggest that Americans would be much more interested in studying history if it involved giving them a chance to interpret and make sense of the past, especially in relation to social identities and power over time.

Unlike the 1619 Project or *Hamilton*, many history classrooms rarely focus on race and other social identities, and how those social identities have had a major role in shaping our current society (Au, 2009; Epstein, 2000, 2009; King, 2017; King & Brown, 2014). When they do focus on race, it is typically only in a handful of units, such as slavery and abolition, European imperialism in Africa, or the modern civil rights movement, with the same being true for gender (i.e., women's suffrage, women's liberation, the reign of women monarchs, such as Cleopatra or Queen Victoria) and class (i.e., turn-of-the-20th-century immigration, unionism), and we much more rarely see lessons on sexual orientation (i.e., gay liberation movement, legalization of same-sex marriage) and never on transgender history (Martell & Stevens, 2017b, 2018). We argue that if the history classroom focused on race, gender, class, sexual orientation, and other social identities, we would not see routine news headlines like the following:

- "High School History Doesn't Have to Be Boring" (Cutler, 2014)
- "Why Do Students Hate History?" (Milo, 2015)
- "Why So Many Students Hate History—and What to Do About It" (Strauss, 2017)
- "Why Are Fewer People Majoring in History?" (Daley, 2018)

Instead, history would be not only one of the most popular school (and university) disciplines, but also one that students felt had importance in their daily lives and involved real-world applications. We argue that a focus on social identity and movement building is a needed shift in making the subject relevant to students (and citizens).

MAKING THE CURRICULUM MULTICULTURAL AND CRITICAL

There are many overlapping and competing definitions of curriculum. Caswell and Campbell (1935) defined curriculum as "all the experiences children have under the guidance of teachers" (p. 69). Some decades later, Schwab (1983) offered a different definition: "what is successfully conveyed to differing degrees to different students, by committed teachers using appropriate materials and actions" (p. 240). Traditionally, curriculum was defined as all of the materials and actions that guide learning. In these definitions, the teacher is typically the person who creates the curriculum. However, numerous democratic and critical educators have argued that curriculum is, and must be, co-constructed by teachers *and* students (Brough, 2012; Duncan-Andrade & Morrell, 2008; Paris & Alim, 2017; Picower, 2012). As such, we define the history curriculum as all of the learning experiences, including materials and activities, that are constructed by teachers and students to further their understanding of history. With that definition of curriculum in mind, we argue that the history curriculum must be multicultural *and* critical. However, first we will explain how curricula may be non-multicultural or liberal in its focus.

Non-Multicultural Curriculum

Traditionally, the history curriculum has been hegemonic and has lacked multicultural perspectives. The history curriculum has maintained White, male, middle-class and wealthy, and heteronormative views of the past (Au, 2009; Chandler & Branscombe, 2015; Crocco, 2001; King & Chandler, 2016; Mayo, 2007; Noddings, 2001). In the United States and elsewhere, the history curriculum has primarily served as a device for supremacy, and particularly White supremacy. As Banks (1998) has described, the purpose of the history curriculum "was to create nation-states in which all groups shared one dominant mainstream culture" (p. 297), and all nondominant groups were expected to relinquish their original cultures to fully participate in the nation-state. People of color, women, the working class and poor, and immigrants were expected to conform to the dominant group's histories, accept the dominant group's narratives of the past, and abandon their perspectives often rooted in their home cultures. It is the reason why so many world history courses (sometimes called Western Civilization) start with ancient Greece or Rome, despite much older civilizations predating theirs in places like Africa, Asia, and the Americas. It is the reason why so many U.S. history courses begin with European colonization, rather than the Indigenous people's history before colonization.

For example, Banks (1998) described his own upbringing as an African American in the Arkansas Delta in the 1950s. He explained his difficulty reconciling the representation of African Americans portrayed in his textbooks with the people he knew in his family and community. While the textbook portrayed happy and loyal enslaved people and only a few African American success stories (such as Booker T. Washington, George Washington Carver, and Marian Anderson), he knew many personal success stories and examples of resistance to racial segregation within his community; the two narratives did not square. This experience continued through college, as it was not until Banks went to graduate school that he first began reading a significant number of Black authors and Black histories.

This story is not uncommon. Many students (and especially White students) continue to receive a non-multicultural history curriculum. They learn all of their history from dominant lenses, or what Paris and Alim (2017), using the work of Morrison (1998), described as through White, patriarchal, cisheteronormative, English-monolingual, ableist, classist, xenophobic, Judeo-Christian gazes. Relatedly, Sleeter (2011) has referred to the school curriculum in the United States as Euro-American studies; we would agree that this tends to apply to most history curricula. To be multicultural, a history curriculum must search for, examine, and write histories not exclusively (or almost exclusively) from dominant groups. It also means not positioning nondominant narratives within dominant frames. For example, many history teachers portray only the White image of Martin Luther King Jr. and share his more popular quotes (such as his speech during the March on Washington) that often focus on tolerance, rather than the vast majority of his speeches or letters, which present a more radical message and one where he directly questions White supremacy, violence, war, and lack of support for the poor.

Liberal Multicultural Curriculum

Since the 1960s, there has been a steady increase in the amount of multicultural content in the history curriculum; however, much of this multicultural history curriculum has not been critical, and instead it has shown history through a primarily liberal lens. May and Sleeter (2010) have described liberal multiculturalism as focusing "on getting along better, primarily via a greater recognition of, and respect for, ethnic, cultural, and/or linguistic differences" (p. 4). It is a problem-solving approach to race, where diversity is seen as a problem, rather than an asset. It often trivializes and essentializes diversity, where the focus is on celebration of cultures, and it often presents cultures in monolithic ways. This approach typically uses what Noddings (2001) called an "add women and stir" view of curriculum (or what we would describe more broadly as "add diversity and stir"). Perspectives of nondominant groups are simply an add-on to the mainstream curriculum to showcase the dominant group's experiences. Moreover, it depoliticizes culture by ignoring the relationship between dominant identities and power in society. Liberal multiculturalism overemphasizes the individual and de-emphasizes the role of social systems in inequity.

This type of curriculum has grown in popularity as a response to the increasing student population in the United States and elsewhere. It allows teachers, and specifically teachers from dominant groups, to feel good about diversity. It is a celebration of diversity without the tough conversations needed around inequity and injustice. While Black History Month was origi-nally created by Carter G. Woodson to challenge the White curriculum, and some teachers do use it to critically examine racial injustice and inequity (King, 2017; King & Brown, 2014), it has been used by many teachers (espe-cially White teachers) to protect the status quo and to relegate learning about Black history to 1 month a year. During this month, teachers often present an essentialized narrative or a single story of the Black experience (often overemphasizing Martin Luther King Jr.'s less controversial speeches and de-emphasizing the importance of the people organized within a larger civil rights movement). Not surprisingly, when you ask students at the end of the month to describe the Black history, they will often say it started with slavery and ended with Martin Luther King Jr.'s assassination (and something like "how one man changed the world"). They will describe Rosa Parks as just a single individual (usually an old and tired one, which is inaccurate) who stood up for her own personal rights (instead of being an activist working on behalf of a larger movement of people). These are prime examples of liberal multiculturalism. They emphasize individualism, meritocracy, and tolerance. They do not challenge the current structures of society, and they send the message that the answer to oppression is asking people to make better indi-vidual choices or to stop participating in discrimination.

Critical Multicultural Curriculum

Our conception of critical multicultural history is rooted in the work of May and Sleeter (2010) and Nieto (2000). May and Sleeter (2010) argued that critical multiculturalism aims to build solidarity across diverse com-munities, which can only happen when there is a collective struggle against oppression in all forms. It is how social activists approach studying the past, by focusing on social change and liberation. It involves not only simply cel-ebrating cultural differences, but also naming and challenging social inequ-ity in relation to race, class, gender, sexual orientation, religion, and other social identities. If the curriculum is to be a tool for justice, then it must present a critical multicultural perspective, giving "priority to structural analysis of unequal power relationships, analyzing the role of institutional inequities, including but not necessarily limited to racism" (May & Sleeter, 2010, p. 10). It must also be a source for decolonizing and globalizing the history content (Merryfield & Subedi, 2006; Subedi, 2013; Tejeda et al., 2003) by considering how colonization, settlerism, and Eurocentrism have shaped the world's past and present. Additionally, Nieto (1994) argued that liberal multiculturalism overly focuses on tolerance, or learning to live together, which is a "low level of multicultural support, reflecting as it does an acceptance of the *status quo* with but slight accommodations for difference" (p. 9). Instead, she argued that teachers must move from acceptance to respect and solidarity, which involves critiquing social arrangements based on race and other social identities. Building on this, we have argued that history teachers should work to build equity-oriented classrooms, rather than tolerance-oriented ones, where they emphasize helping students understand how race and other social identities have led to the creation of systems of advantage in the past and present day (Martell, 2017; Martell & Stevens, 2017b). We use Table 4.1 to describe the different types of history curricula and how history teachers can make their curricula more critical and multicultural. This may provide guidance for teachers and students in creating critical multicultural history curricula.

Our conception of critical multicultural history is also rooted in culturally relevant and sustaining pedagogy. We have described culturally sustaining pedagogy (CSP; Ladson-Billings, 2014; Paris, 2012; Paris & Alim, 2014, 2017) elsewhere as:

> an updated version of, or as Ladson-Billings (2014) put it, a "remix" of, culturally relevant pedagogy (CRP; Ladson-Billings, 1995a, 1995b, 2006). It is an innovation of CRP, but in a way that still retains many of its original qualities (in the same way that a new track in hip-hop may revitalize an older track). The remix to the original theory does not imply that the prior was deficient; rather, it updates it in a way that speaks to evolving needs. (Martell & Stevens, 2019)

Built on Ladson-Billings's (1995a, 1995b, 2014) groundbreaking work, teachers who employ CSP, much like CRP, center their classrooms on students' academic success, nurturing and supporting their cultural competence and developing their sociopolitical and critical consciousness (which may be the most important component and one that is often missed by teachers and researchers). Culturally sustaining teachers also focus their energy on empowering their students to define, redefine, and sustain their own cultures, especially when those cultures may be under attack or experiencing destruction from dominant groups (hegemony).

It is not enough to include multicultural voices and perspectives in the history curriculum. Instead, the critical multicultural history curriculum must spotlight how racism, sexism, classism, homophobia, and other forms of oppression and discrimination have influenced history, which, in turn,

Table 4.1. Types of History Curricula

Non-Multicultural	Liberal Multicultural	Critical Multicultural
Narratives of the past are presented from primarily White, patriarchal, cisheteronormative, English-monolingual, ableist, classist, xenophobic, Judeo-Christian lenses.	Narratives of the past are presented from people of color and women; LGBTQ, multilingual, and dis/able people; poor and working classes; immigrants; and people of faiths other than Christianity, but with a tolerance orientation.	Narratives of the past are presented from people of color and women; LGBTQ people; multilingual people; people with dis/abilities poor and working classes; immigrants; and people of faiths other than Christianity, but with an equity orientation.
Lessons rarely use sources or other materials from the perspectives of nondominant groups, and those groups are usually portrayed through dominant lenses.	Lessons regularly use sources or other materials from the perspectives of nondominant groups, but typically include single sources or essentialize their experiences (do not show the complexity and contrasting views found within a particular group).	Lessons regularly use sources or other materials from the perspectives of nondominant groups, and typically include multiple sources highlighting experiences in authentic ways (show the complexity and contrasting views found within a particular group).
Curriculum is constructed solely by teachers; students have no choice in what they study.	Curriculum is constructed mostly by teachers; students have limited choice in what they study.	Curriculum is co-constructed by teachers and students; students have significant choice in what they study.

has led us to the present and will ultimately shape the future. Teachers must include thoughtful considerations of whose voices are and are not included in the curriculum, but they must also afford students regular opportunities to include their own voices (and those of their ancestors and people who share their identities) within the curriculum (An, 2020; Au, 2009; Busey, 2014; Busey & Cruz, 2015; Khan et al., 2020; King, 2016; King et al., 2012; King et al., 2014; King & Womac, 2014; King & Woodson, 2017; Rodríguez, 2018; Santiago, 2017; Woodson, 2015, 2016). Moreover, the critical multicultural history curriculum avoids an "add diversity and stir" view of curriculum. The perspectives of the oppressed and members of non-dominant groups are not an add-on. Rather, they are essential for an accurate and authentic telling and retelling of the past.

There is strong evidence that students benefit from a critical multi-cultural curriculum and teachers' use of culturally relevant and sustaining pedagogy. Sleeter (2012) found numerous small-scale studies that showed increased student success. Building on that work, Aronson and Laughter (2016) reviewed 37 studies on culturally relevant education across the content areas and found that students in CRP- and CSP-oriented classrooms reported increased engagement and motivation, better abilities to understand different cultural perspectives of content, an increased ability to draw connections between students' lives inside and outside the classroom, and increased student learning (including correlations with increased student scores on standardized tests, which are not necessarily good measures of student learning). Relatedly, Sleeter's (2011) review of research on ethnic studies programs (which typically include the study of ethnic histories) found similar results, with three overlapping impacts: increased academic engagement, increased academic achievement, and increased personal empowerment. Moreover, Sleeter's review found that students of color were aware of dominant biases in their curricula and could describe these biases in some detail, and these students desired a curriculum that better aligned with their lived experiences.

Building on the work of Ayers and colleagues (2009), we argue that critical multicultural history classrooms focus on three principles: equity, activism and movements, and social identities. As teachers and students cocreate their classrooms, they consider how past events did or did not contribute to fairness and justice. They contemplate the role of activists and movements in past events. They deliberate on how social identities and group membership have resulted in privilege for some at the expense of others, and how they have formed the foundation of structural racism, sexism, classism, homophobia and cisheterosexism, and nativism. Within each of the following sections, we offer potential questions that students should ask while engaging in the history curriculum to ensure they are centering justice.

Principle 1. Equity

The first principle of critical multicultural history classrooms focuses on equity in past and present societies. Ayers and colleagues (2009) described their definition of equity or fairness as demanding that what is afforded to the most privileged people in a society must be the standard for all, which includes redressing and repairing historical and embedded injustices. A critical multicultural history curriculum includes regular examinations of inequity, and especially how inequity was built into the system over time. Intentionally, like many other scholars, we use the term inequity, rather than inequality, here. Equality implies a state of everyone receiving equal, while equity strives for fairness; those who need more should receive more. To focus on equity, teachers and students should be continually asking of each event that they study: Did this event increase or decrease inequity or injustice? If so, how?

Principle 2. Activism and Movements

The second principle of critical multicultural classrooms focuses on activism and movements in past and present societies. Ayers and colleagues (2009) described their definition of activism or agency as involving a full participation of people to see, understand, and, when necessary, change all before them. A critical multicultural history curriculum frames events around groups and movements, rather than individuals (for more information on thinking like an activist, see Chapter 2). It highlights the collective work of activists to achieve social change. As Zinn (2002) argued, movement leaders are only the figureheads allowed to represent the larger masses of people. While individuals are important, and undoubtedly many sources that students use are created by individuals, teachers and students will be aware that these voices only represent one perspective and do not speak for the entire group. A critical multicultural history curriculum emphasizes that in any historical analysis, it is crucial to triangulate sources to ensure that they accurately represent individuals and the groups to which they belong. Teachers and students should be continually asking of each event that they study: During this event, did activists and movements demand change? Did they accomplish that change (and to what extent)?

Principle 3. Social Identities

The third principle of critical multicultural classrooms focuses on social identities in past and present societies. Ayers and colleagues (2009) described their definition of social literacy or relevance as resisting the effects of materialism and consumerism, as well as resisting the power of social evils rooted in forms of supremacy (i.e., White supremacy, patriarchy, homophobia), while nourishing individual social identities and connections with others and understanding how everyone's lives are negotiated within preestablished power relationships. A critical multicultural history curriculum centers identity and specifically spotlights the narratives of nondominant groups. When selecting sources or other materials for inquiries, teachers and students will intentionally challenge if there are important voices missing. They will search for multiple sources from within a particular social group, and if those sources are unavailable (since certain groups have been intentionally left out or removed from the historical record), they will use their historical imagination to consider possible perspectives. By doing this, the history classroom serves as a place for students to confront examples of cultural hegemony and understand the experiences of those groups whose histories have been framed by dominant lenses. Teachers and students should be continually asking of each event that they study: Did certain groups experience this event differently? Were there different perspectives of this event within groups? How and why?

CRITICAL MULTICULTURALISM IN ACTION

In this section, we provide one model for teachers who want a more holistic approach to incorporating critical multiculturalism in their classrooms. This section describes the process that two teachers went through to rewrite their U.S. history curriculum, which intentionally centered the voices of Indigenous, Black, and queer people from the past. In order for other teachers to replicate their work, we have outlined the steps that they took and the major changes that they made.

Step 1: Thinking About Students

Ms. Becca Luther, who is a White history teacher at an urban high school outside Boston, Massachusetts, ran into a former student who was then enrolled at a local university. The student explained that she was taking an African American history course and it was the first time she was actually interested in history, because she could finally see herself in the curriculum. This was a powerful moment for Ms. Luther, because, as a teacher, she was considered by colleagues as someone who was exemplary in her inclusion of diverse voices in the curriculum. Yet, in speaking with her former student, she realized that while her curriculum might be more inclusive, she might simply be adding nondominant voices to the dominant narratives of the past. In many ways, she was implementing an "add diversity and stir" approach to her students' study of the past. In contrast, her former student was describing what it felt like to have a course that centered the experiences of her family and ancestors within the main narrative. This moment forced Ms. Luther to reflect deeply on how she was presenting those different voices in her curriculum. She asked: How can I better design my units of study around nondominant groups' narratives? What would it look like to rewrite the curriculum centering Indigenous, Black, and queer voices from U.S. history?

In the midst of her reflection, the high school's Black Student Union gave a presentation to several groups of teachers about how they were feeling disconnected from the content of their history classes. The students were concerned not only because there was a lack of representation in the curriculum, but also because there were fewer Black students (and other students of color) enrolled in the so-called higher-level classes (advanced placement and honors classes were predominantly comprised of White and upper-middle-class students). The students helped Ms. Luther realize that the two problems were related, which inspired her to embark on a complete overhaul of the U.S. history curriculum, starting with asking the students what they would like to learn. Simultaneously, she began working with her department colleagues to create a program to better recruit and support students of color in higher-level classes. Her view was that more challenging courses should not only actively recruit more students of color, but also change the way they are taught to be more relevant and engaging. This would hopefully increase the number of students of color and help them successfully complete the courses.

Ms. Luther began by implementing a survey in her current history classes on what students wanted to learn, and she focused on the answers from the students of color. From the results, it was clear that students of color did not want their identities to be a sidebar in the curriculum, nor did they want their people to be portrayed as victims. The students shared that their experiences learning about Black, Latinx, Asian, or Indigenous history were often organized around moments of oppression, such as slavery or the taking of land by White settlers. When there were triumphs and acts of resistance, they were often oversimplified. The students did not want to only learn about a small group of leaders from their communities (Martin Luther King Jr., Cesar Chavez, etc.). They wanted to learn how ordinary people of color resisted oppression, worked for social change, and achieved their objectives. They wanted to know how the different views within communities of color impacted their histories. This became the starting point for Ms. Luther's curriculum revision.

Step 2: Finding Support and Mapping Guiding Principles

Ms. Luther knew she could not do this work alone, and she began to look for collaborators. She discovered that one of her colleagues, Ms. Dana Silva, a Brazilian American teacher at the same school, was simultaneously doing this work on her own. They met and began planning. Together, they created two goals: (a) to weave together different narratives from history to create a more accurate representation of all people; and (b) to center voices of color, so that the curriculum reflects all of the students in their classrooms. They knew that if students, and especially students of color, could see themselves in the main narratives of the curriculum, they would become more engaged. They went to their department chair, who supported their work. Next, they received a small amount of funds to attend a professional development workshop on teaching local Native nations in the history classroom. There, Ms. Luther and Ms. Silva worked with a local Nipmuc activist to redesign their curriculum on pre- and post-European settlement in New England. They described it as a powerful moment, which helped them confront the traditional White narrative of settlement in Massachusetts. This would be the start of their creation of a new curriculum map, which they would pilot and then present to their colleagues as a replacement for the current Eurocentric course of study.

Ms. Luther and Ms. Silva also knew that they must look beyond the textbook and traditional sources, as Indigenous people were often excluded or erased from the historical record. To do this, they were able to have two guest speakers from the Indigenous Canadian organization KAIROS (KAIROS Canada, 2019) work with their department colleagues. KAIROS is a participatory program that teaches over 500 years of history through a blanket created by Indigenous Elders. This professional development was a powerful moment for the teachers of the department, as it introduced new historical people and events from the past, but it also had them question what counts as primary sources. Moreover, it offered a model example of centering Indigenous perspectives in the telling of American history.

It became clear to Ms. Luther and Ms. Silva that this work required more than just adding a few lessons on each missing group; rather, they needed to rethink what lessons should be included altogether. If they were to decolonize the history curriculum, all of the units of their U.S. history course would need to be told around the Indigenous stories (their course covered from before Columbus to after the Civil War); White people would be the "add and stir" group in the curriculum. Moreover, all lessons would need to involve Indigenous voices and perspectives. Eurocentric history depicts Indigenous people as passive bystanders while Whites dominated and destroyed their way of life. This is intentional, as it helps maintain a narrative that the destruction of the Indigenous people was inevitable, and it validates the decisions made by Europeans in the past (Dunbar-Ortiz, 2015). Traditionally, school history has neglected to show the many different ways that Indigenous people survived and resisted. Ms. Luther and Ms. Silva began with this as their guiding principle for the curriculum (re)build.

Step 3: (Re)Building the Curriculum

Ms. Luther and Ms. Silva began by searching for new materials that authentically represented Indigenous voices. They searched more traditional online resources, such as the National Archives and the Smithsonian, and they also searched the museums, libraries, and repositories of various Native nations and the National Congress of American Indians. They reached out to local organizations, like the Institute for New England Native American Studies at the University of Massachusetts Boston and the Mashpee Wampanoag Indian Museum. Next, based on their research, they created a list of the events of most historical importance to Native people before and during the arrival of European settlers. They used these events to organize the chronology of the curriculum. They then placed various primary and secondary sources within their timeline, with a particular emphasis on those sources that highlighted the Indigenous perspective. They found that the overarching theme across the curriculum was survival and resistance. The purpose of the unit was to show how Indigenous people preserved and maintained their communities, and the unit would also highlight their organizations, languages, and religions. The White narrative would be present in the unit, but in a way that emphasized the concept of settler colonialism. Finally, Ms. Luther and Ms. Silva divided the work of taking those primary and secondary sources and building engaging lesson plans around them. They aimed to create powerful lesson plans that included thought-provoking inquiry questions, engaging openers, and in-depth examinations of documents and arguments that focused on the experience of Indigenous people. In the following subsections, we highlight some of the major changes Ms. Luther and Ms. Silva made in the curriculum around the core principles of a justice-oriented history curriculum: equity, activism and movements, and social identities (Ayers et al., 2009).

Equity. Throughout the rebuilt U.S. history curriculum, students focused on unpacking how history contributed to the social construction of race and other social identities. Additionally, they analyzed the systematic privileges that some social groups held (and continue to hold). To begin the year, Ms. Luther and Ms. Silva had students analyze their own identity through researching their family and their backgrounds. The classes participated in activities where they explored their own identities, including race, gender, class, religion, dis/ability, and citizenship. Students were asked to consider how their home cultures framed how they viewed the world differently than others. Students were also asked to consider the ways that their families experienced privilege or oppression in the past and present. They learned about intersectionality and how oppression can be amplified by being a member of multiple minoritized groups.

The students were then exposed to different Native cultures. They first participated in several activities that explored relatively mundane aspects of daily life, such as food, festivals, and art, in an attempt to help the students (most of whom were not Indigenous) begin to see the similarities and differences between their traditions and those of Native people. In this unit, Ms. Luther and Ms. Silva very intentionally included a diverse array of Native groups, so students would not see Indigenous people as monolithic. Once students had a surface-level understanding of several Native nations, the teachers then had them dig deeper and think about how Native people may think about race, gender, class, language, sexual orientation, and religion.

At the beginning of the course, the students engaged in lessons about the history of White supremacy and how it played a role in the creation of the English American colonies, as well as how it framed Europeans' understandings of Indigenous (and African) peoples. They learned that race is an imagined human construct, and they read research on a lack of genetic differences between people of different races. They read articles that discussed how race and Indigenousness are overlapping concepts with important differences. This included how Europeans placed their conceptions of race on Native people and how they attempted to change Indigenous people to fit their conceptions of Whiteness (e.g., Indian praying towns, federal reservation system, Indian boarding schools). The classes read articles about the cultural and linguistic diversity within the Native peoples of the Americans. Many students were surprised and began to question much of their understanding about race and Indigenousness, allowing them to also question other aspects of their current world, including gender and class differences. Many of the Latinx students began to think of their own Indigenous ancestors and how they may have been erased from their family's histories.

Activism and movements. Throughout the rebuilt U.S. history curriculum, students were asked to analyze history through social movements and activism. Ms. Luther and Ms. Silva rarely framed protests or resistance as "revolts," but instead as uprisings, rebellions, or revolutions. They also highlighted the role of Native people within other uprisings, rebellions, or revolutions that are often seen as White (such as the American Revolution). For example, typically in the history curriculum, students will learn about "Tecumseh's War" (a label framed by Whites, which positions Tecumseh as causing the war). However, Ms. Luther and Ms. Silva reframed it as "Tecumseh's Uprising" with a lesson that connected Tecumseh's actions to White violations of treaties with Native people and the White supremacist underpinnings of laws in the United States. Students used the film *We Shall Remain: Tecumseh's Vision* and primary sources, including Tecumseh's speeches, to analyze his confederacy's resistance and if it was a good model for future Native resistance movements. The mini-unit ended with students designing a memorial to recognize Tecumseh's contributions to U.S. history, which would elevate his status to that of other American leaders. At the same time, Ms. Luther and Ms. Silva were careful to not diminish the voices of other people of color in the U.S. history curriculum. Later in the year, the students would learn about slave rebellions and slave autobiographies as forms of resistance. Again, this highlighted the power of movements over individual acts in the past. Students read the graphic novel *The Life of Frederick Douglass*, viewed portions of the film *12 Years a Slave*, and participated in several lessons where they examined historical sources from the Stono Rebellion, Nat Turner's Rebellion, and Prosser's Rebellion. In these studies, the students examined the complex relationships between enslaved African Americans and Native people, which included solidarity but also moments where White leaders pitted the groups against each other. This unit also included a lesson about the role of many Indigenous nations in providing refuge for runaway enslaved people, including various local Indigenous nations in Massachusetts.

Social identities. Throughout the rebuilt U.S. history curriculum, the teachers worked to ensure multiple identities were incorporated within each lesson. Ms. Luther and Ms. Silva designed numerous lessons across the curriculum to show the complexities within past and present Indigenous communities related to social identities. Students examined historical documents that showed how the Haudenosaunee (Iroquois) had a matriarchal society with women responsible for political and social decisionmaking. They read an article on the Diné (Navajo) and watched a video on the Passamaquoddy (a nation located in Maine, which is about an hour away from their high school) people's historical conceptions of sexual orientation and transgender people, including the concept of Two-Spirit as a third gender. The students read research on a lack of the word "disability" within many Native languages and how most Native groups generally lacked a deficit view of people with dis/abilities that was brought to the Americas by Europeans. Ms. Luther created a lesson on Lewis and Clark's ethnocentrism toward Indigenous women (including a misconception that Hidatsa men led agriculture, resulting in several problems, such as the destruction of their corn mill), which may have influenced the little credit that they gave to Sacagawea for her leadership and efforts during their expedition. Ms. Silva designed a lesson around an article she found that showed the impacts of the government-forced Indian boarding schools on Native cultures today.

Ms. Luther and Ms. Silva also included the voices of LGBTQ people throughout each unit, which helped students see that Indigenous people had different views of sexual orientation and gender—and how this was also the case for other groups who were in the Americas. In one lesson, they had the students read an excerpt from Bronski's (2019) *A Queer History of the United States for Young People* to challenge the traditionally held ideas that all Puritans had the same strict Christian beliefs and there were no dissenters among them. The students read about Publick Universal Friend, who was genderless, which included abandoning their birth name and gendered pronouns. Ms. Luther and Ms. Silva believed it was incredibly important, especially for their LGBTQ students, to see examples of people with similar sexual orientations and gender identities in the past.

Ultimately, Ms. Luther and Ms. Silva's rebuild of the U.S. history curriculum was successful in better centering Indigenous voices. While the process did provide challenges, such as a lack of readily available primary source documents, their work paid off. After teaching this new curriculum for the year, both teachers saw important changes in their students. Their students were more likely to ask questions about the Indigenous peoples' experience during early American history. Some began to see their own family's histories as connected to Native people in the past and present. Most importantly, they began to see history as much more relevant. The students developed a historical context for their current world. They now saw Indigenous nations as complex groups of people who were not just victims—they were resistors, who persist and continue to sustain their communities.

CHAPTER 5

Transformative Democratic Citizenship

One of the most important purposes of history education (and schooling more broadly) is to enable people to make present-day civic decisions. We study the past, because it contextualizes the decisions citizens* must make in the present. As Stearns (1998) argued, "Studying history helps us understand how recent, current, and prospective changes that affect the lives of citizens are emerging or may emerge and what causes are involved" (p. 5). However, any citizenship education must also prepare local, national, and global citizens for the multicultural world and nations in which we live. Banks (2002) argued, "Unity without diversity results in cultural repression and hegemony. Diversity without unity leads to Balkanization and the fracturing of the nation-state" (p. 133). We cannot fully realize democracy until all people in those democracies have equity and justice.

Today we may be experiencing that fracturing of a nation-state. We are seeing the product of centuries of democratic education without multicultural education, especially critical multicultural education (discussed at length in Chapter 4). Domestically and abroad, there have been increasing numbers of violent acts inspired by White supremacy, Christian supremacy (especially targeting Jewish, Muslim, and Sikh people), homophobia, and the hatred of women and trans people (Femincide Watch, 2019; Hassan, 2019; Human Rights Campaign Foundation, 2019). Even when it does not rise to the level of violence, people from nondominant groups face discrimination in their daily lives and a lack of opportunity in society (Harvard Opinion Research Program, 2018). We now live in a society that is perhaps more inequitable than ever before and clearly more inequitable than just a generation ago (Kochhar & Cilluffo, 2018). This oppression was built into the United States' foundation, as the nation was founded on slavery and a lack of citizenship for women and Black, Indigenous, and other people of

---

*Throughout this book, we use "citizens" broadly to include all members within local, national, or global communities with civic responsibility, regardless of their state-determined citizenship status, which often excludes documented and undocumented immigrants, as well as members of politically marginalized groups.

color. Yet those oppressive structures built into the democracy are not fixed; the power of democracy is that the people can change their societies. The history classroom can serve as the key space for this important citizenship education.

For many Americans, especially White, male, straight, and cisgender Americans, society's oppressive structures are invisible (and that is by design). Their history education has been one of the most important devices used to obscure those oppressive structures and to maintain the status quo. History education has traditionally been used to justify and uphold current power arrangements (Banks, 2004; Ladson-Billings, 2003). As such, mainstream history serves as a tool to convince dominant groups that they have received their social privileges fairly, and other peoples' disadvantages are deserved. For example, mainstream U.S. history generally includes a narrative that turn-of-the-20th-century White immigrants pulled themselves up by their bootstraps, which led to their social success. Yet this is in stark contrast to a counter-narrative that portrays their success as the outcome of changing conceptions of Whiteness, which eventually elevated their status in society (often at the expense of people of color), which was later cemented economically with social programs such as the New Deal and the GI Bill (Bartholomew & Reumschuessel, 2018; Jacobson, 1999; Roediger, 2006), with both government programs including embedded advantages for Whites (such as housing preferences and limited or missing benefits for soldiers of color).

Moreover, since many members of our society have been intentionally excluded from the democracy, they have experienced what Banks (2017) described as failed citizenship:

> when individuals or groups who are born within a nation or migrate to it and live within it for an extended period of time do not internalize the values and ethos of the nation-state, feel structurally excluded within it, and have highly ambivalent feeling toward it. (p. 367)

He argued that schools, and their history classrooms, contribute to this failed citizenship when they use "assimilationist approaches to civic education that requir[e] minoritized students from diverse groups to deny their home cultures and languages" (p. 367). As such, teaching the past from assimilationist lenses is antithetical to a true democratic society.

If learning communities, including the history classroom, are to be tools for justice, they should be built around fostering a transformative democratic citizenship, which Banks (2017) defined as "the ability to implement and promote policies, actions, and changes that are consistent with values such as human rights, social justice, and equality" (p. 367). It is the ability of *all* citizens to know and be able to influence and challenge those with power in the democracy (and to have the opportunity to *be* those people in power). Banks (2015) argued that transformative democratic citizenship education must "challenge some of the key epistemological assumptions of mainstream academic knowledge . . . [it] assumes that knowledge is not neutral, is influenced by human interests, and reflects the power relationships within society" (p. 154). As Lévesque (2008) had similarly argued, history education "can make an important contribution to democratic citizenship. Historical knowledge of political, social, cultural, and economic systems overlaps with the democratic knowledge necessary for active citizenship . . . [to] more effectively engage in democratic society" (p. 28). Aligned with this idea, Banks (2017) argued that history teaching must "help students from marginalized groups become recognized and participatory citizens by attaining a sense of structural integration and inclusion within their nation-states and clarified national identities" (p. 373).

History classrooms must be places that help students develop a sociopolitical consciousness and cultural competence, which are essential citizenship skills in any multicultural state (Ladson-Billings, 1995, 2006, 2014). School, and history classrooms, should also be a place to help students, especially students of color and other marginalized groups, define, redefine, and sustain their cultures (Ladson-Billings, 2014; Paris, 2012; Paris & Alim, 2017). It is important that any citizenship education focuses on the overlap between multiculturalism and democracy (Marri, 2005) and decenters Whiteness (Oto & Chikkatur, in press), especially within history classrooms (Martinelle et al., 2019). Within history classrooms, learning communities should be focused on understanding how citizenship has been denied to many, with the goal of creating a democracy that is open to all and based on principles of justice. It should model democratic ideas and practices, and it should be a place for students to engage in active citizenship. It should foster what Westheimer and Kahne (2004) called justice-oriented citizens, which can be defined as citizens who know how to "examine social, political, and economic structures and explore strategies for change that address root causes of the problem" (Westheimer, 2015, p. 40). For example, while some citizens may volunteer to organize a food drive (which Westheimer described as participatory citizenship), justice-oriented citizens will also ask, "Why are people hungry?" and will act on ways to address that social problem more systematically.

We argue that if history classrooms are to genuinely focus on transformative democratic citizenship, they must include the study of history that is political (but not partisan), democratic, and multicultural. By focusing on these concepts, students are more likely to develop the types of thinking skills about the past that will help them make informed decisions in the present as citizens. Moreover, it will help them understand the complicated and often invisible social structures that govern our democratic system, and will offer them ways of studying the past that might help inform the future.

STUDYING A POLITICAL, BUT NONPARTISAN, HISTORY

The study of history is never neutral. All history is ideological and, as such, also political. Those who claim it is not mask their ideology. As Zinn (2002) wrote of studying history, "You can't be neutral on a moving train . . . the events are already moving in certain deadly directions, and to be neutral means to accept that" (p. 8). We study history because it helps us understand our present, and it informs the decisions that we make as citizens about our shared future. It is important to acknowledge that the history that we study is embedded with political ideas and is framed by ideological narratives. The ideologies of the past and the present serve as the structures for how we make sense of history. Those who claim they do not, intentionally or unintentionally, mask their ideology and their politics.

Yet, while all history is political, history is not partisan. When we say partisan, we mean to be prejudiced toward considering one specific interpretation as the only interpretation, based on a blind allegiance to a particular party or group. Some political scientists have described this as political tribalism (Hawkins et al., 2018). In this logic, tribes demand loyalty at all costs, even when those costs may be destructive or antidemocratic (Packer, 2018). History, including recent history, offers numerous examples of how partisanship (and especially extreme partisanship) can destroy societies, especially democratic societies (Hawkins et al., 2018; Levitsky & Ziblatt, 2018). However, there are also examples, such as Chile in the 1990s, where overcoming partisanship can lead to a restoration of democracy (Levitsky & Ziblatt, 2018). Partisan history involves disregarding all narratives that do not conform to your own preferred ideologies. It also means seeking only evidence that validates your preferred historical narrative, rather than searching for historical evidence that might put into question that same historical narrative. Students of history must seek evidence that supports, but might also put into question, their preferred ideological historical narratives.

Moreover, justice is nonpartisan. For us to survive as a society, we all must be continually seeking justice. While we may have different political beliefs or conceptions of how to achieve this, ultimately seeking a more just and fair society must be the main goal of citizenship, education, and specifically history education. The Preamble to the U.S. Constitution (1787) is explicit in this:

> We the people of the United States, in order to form a more perfect union, *establish justice*, [italics added] insure domestic tranquility, provide for the common defense, promote the general welfare, and secure the blessings of liberty to ourselves and our posterity.

In fact, James Madison (1788), a key framer of the Constitution, wrote in Federalist 51, "Justice is the end of government. It is the end of civil society.

It ever has been and ever will be pursued until it be obtained, or until liberty be lost in the pursuit." If history education is preparation for citizenship, then it must be focused on understanding how justice was sought in the past and is still being sought today.

Partisanship

Partisanship is a significant political dilemma of our time, especially here in the United States (however, we would also argue it is not unique to our time or location; there have been many highly partisan eras in the past, and the term itself dates back to the 16th century). As facets of our society (politicians, the media, and subsequently citizens themselves) appear to be becoming increasingly partisan in the last several decades (e.g., the increasing popularity of Fox News, MSNBC, and other news outlets that serve a primarily partisan purpose), simultaneously political scientists are also documenting a weakening of our democratic institutions that might be related (Levitsky & Ziblatt, 2018). This increasing partisanization has impacted history education as well; granted, it appears, so far, to be only a few relatively isolated events. In separate instances, former Indiana governor Mitch Daniels and an Arkansas legislator attempted to ban the use of books by Howard Zinn in schools (Clauss, 2017; Ohlheiser, 2013). The conservative talk show host Rush Limbaugh created a series of history books for children to show his view of U.S. history as the only correct one (Friedersdorf, 2014). These examples involve political actors describing their particular narratives of history as telling the truth (free from political tampering) of the past. Yet these narratives are clearly rooted in conservative interpretation of the past (Chumley, 2013; Friedersdorf, 2014). Partisan history is tantamount to propaganda. It is important that students are not banned from accessing historical writings deemed "dangerous" by politicians due to their differing ideologies (moreover, this may backfire; after the Arkansas bill gained media attention, hundreds of teachers in the state requested free copies of Zinn's book from the Zinn Education Project). History teachers should be careful to avoid materials that portray only one narrative or cast other narratives as untruthful (which is different from inaccurate; we want to draw that distinction, as students need to be given correct facts). If those materials are used (e.g., some may argue that corporate-produced textbooks are a form of propaganda based on the narratives they include), it is essential that the teacher helps their students understand the embedded political narratives and the ways authors may intentionally hide them for political advantage. For all materials, teachers should prepare students to detect the embedded political narratives and to critically examine those narratives.

A history education that intentionally forefronts political ideologies can serve as part of the antidote for partisan history. We argue that helping students see the difference between political (which we think is necessary) and partisan (which we think is destructive for democracy) should be a main goal of history education, and this should be applied to past (and present) events. It is essential that historians, citizens, and students are explicit with the ideological underpinnings of their interpretations, and they should look for those ideological underpinnings in the materials that they use. How one interprets the past will be framed by lived experience. How people in the past created the historical record will be framed around their cultural views (including race, gender, class, etc.), their political views (including liberalism, conservatism, libertarianism, progressivism, socialism, etc.), and their linguistic and cultural differences. This is an asset in understanding the past, as it may help us uncover new angles or ideas about the past and the present. Partisan history does not seek to understand a particular event through a certain lens or lenses; it attempts to contribute to a predetermined (and often dominant) historical narrative for a partisan purpose, often while declaring that the partisan view is the objective or politically neutral telling of the past, and any alternative views of the past are untrue.

Political Neutrality or Objectivity

Those who proclaim that history is politically neutral or objective misunderstand the nature of history. History is written by humans, and thus it is framed by humans' political (cultural, geographical, economic, etc.) views. Historical narratives are framed by their writers' political values and beliefs. Historians have never been neutral arbiters of the past. From the ancient historian Herodotus to the best-selling modern historians Doris Kearns Goodwin and David McCullough, historians' interpretations of the past have always involved purposeful selection of sources, interpretations based on their worldviews, and the creation of narratives influenced by their political values and beliefs (in fact, for centuries, historians have been described by their political ideologies, such as Tory historians, Whig historians, liberal historians, conservative historians, and Marxist historians). We would argue that Howard Zinn's work is an archetype of good political history. In his writing, he worked diligently to make clear his ideological stances of the past (letting readers know that his work is a Marxist interpretation). Instead of discounting conflicting evidence, he often attempted to explain that evidence in relation to his clear political framework (for a different view of this, we suggest reading Wineburg's [2018] recent writings on Zinn). Importantly, the argument that K–12 history teachers should teach, and history students should learn, politically neutral or objective history is often waged by those who defend the status quo and current social power relationships; they will make the claim that anything other than that is politically biased.

Students come to our classrooms with their own political values and beliefs. Those differences must be acknowledged and respected, and, more importantly, teachers must help students recognize how their values and beliefs frame their interpretations of the past, as well as how other peoples' (including historians' in those groups) interpretations of the past are framed by their own values and beliefs. Additionally, education should encourage students to question their values and beliefs, especially in light of the available evidence. In this process, students will develop a stronger sense of politics and history. Moreover, it will help make the study more relevant to students, as they will better understand how it has shaped their current world (including their own values and beliefs).

For instance, depending on their political values and beliefs, looking at the same set of historical evidence, students may interpret the American Revolution differently. This is also true of citizens and historians. Someone with conservative or libertarian views may interpret the colonial revolt as colonists defending their rights to trade and access markets without government interference, or they may interpret it as colonists defending the rights of local communities to preserve their governance against centralized states (historians like George Bancroft, Edmund Morgan, and Stephan Thernstrom have argued this). Someone with liberal views may instead interpret the colonial revolt as the colonists' attempt to establish democratic government and equality in what became a new nation (historians like Bernard Bailyn and Gordon Wood side with this interpretation). Someone with radical or progressive views may interpret the revolt as an attempt by those with power in the colonies, predominantly merchants and wealthy landowners (including many enslavers), to defend their personal financial interests (historians like Charles Beard and Howard Zinn fall into this camp). In fact, many history teachers have posed the following important (and political) inquiry question to their class: How revolutionary was the American Revolution? Students (and historians) have a range of answers based on their political views. None of these views of the American Revolution are wrong; rather, they take the evidence of the period and analyze it using different ideological frameworks. What is wrong is when students are given only one political framework and are told that this specific framework is the lens to use when examining the past, and it is wrong when students are told that the framework is the only lens that should be used to examine the past.

STUDYING A POLITICAL HISTORY THAT IS
DEMOCRATIC AND MULTICULTURAL

As Barton and Levstik (2004) have argued, history should help prepare students not only for citizenship, but also, more specifically, for citizenship in pluralist participatory democracies. As we described at the beginning of the chapter, democracy and diversity must always be linked; we cannot describe democratic education without multicultural education, and vice versa. When you attempt to make something more democratic, you must also ensure that it is critically examining if all groups are being treated fairly.

We find Marri's (2005) framework for a classroom-based multicultural democratic education (CMDE) particularly helpful in ensuring that teaching and learning are both democratic and multicultural. Marri described the purpose of CMDE as using the classroom to work toward transformative civic ends by helping all citizens understand how any democratic learning must also educate for multiculturalism. Teachers should foster critical views of citizenship within students and acknowledge that the common good "might be 'more good' for some than for others" (Vinson, 2001, p. 71). Students may come to different ideas of how to address those inequities, often based on their ideological frameworks, but in a democracy we must, at a minimum, acknowledge that there are inequities and that they must be corrected to ensure that we truly have a democratic society.

Barriers to a Classroom-Based Multicultural Democratic Education

The way school history has been taught includes many barriers to CMDE. We argue that three practices from the history classroom specifically require a more careful consideration, as teachers attempt to build classrooms that foster democratic and multicultural thinking. These practices include memorization, reading other peoples' narratives, and avoiding presentism.

Memorization. If teachers are to help students as democratic citizens, their classrooms should focus on answering important democratic questions, rather than focus on memorizing historical facts. Stearns (1998) argued that the association of history education with memorization dates back to an earlier time

> [when] knowledge of certain historical facts helped distinguish the educated from the uneducated; the person who could reel off the date of the Norman conquest of England (1066) or the name of the person who came up with the theory of evolution at about the same time that Darwin did (Wallace) was deemed superior. (p. 1)

Yet in a world where the Internet allows someone access to most historical names, dates, and places in seconds, this ability seems far less relevant or necessary. However, more importantly, as Banks (2015) argued, the history curriculum has long failed to prepare students for citizenship, because "it focuses heavily on having students memorize historical and political facts, learn the heroic deeds of historical and political leaders" (p. 154), rather than helping students question and take stances on the past. Instead, history education should help "students to develop decision-making and social action skills needed to identify problems within society, clarify their values, and take action to enhance democracy and social justice within their communities, nation, and the world" (Banks, 2015, p. 154). Banks contended that these chosen facts typically represent the histories of those groups in power, and they are usually selected to defend the current status quo. Moreover, they often serve as a tool for White supremacy and other forms of oppression by presenting the dominant group's narratives of the past as the mainstream. Rather than focusing heavily on memorizing facts, we argue that the history classroom should regularly use evidence (which includes fact-finding) when crafting historical narratives and using ideological frameworks.

When the history classroom heavily involves memorization, it also does not help students develop the skills necessary for citizenship in a democracy. Citizens are never asked to memorize facts as part of their work of citizenship (especially in a world where they can recall facts easily on their smartphones); instead, they are asked to interpret the facts in the pursuit of their civic understanding. Additionally, they are asked to judge and sort evidence based on its trustworthiness and to learn how to triangulate sources (cross checking from multiple accounts) to draw a more coherent view of the past. The history classroom should have the same principle at its core. Instead of rote memorization, the history classroom should be one of continual historical fact-finding, narrative analysis, discussion, and debate. Students should be developing their skills of argumentation and interpretation of the past. These skills are needed not only for citizenship, but also, conveniently, for the work of historians (Wineburg, 2018; Wineburg & Reisman, 2015).

Other Peoples' Narratives. If teachers are to help students as democratic citizens, they should engage in the writing of history where they write narratives rooted in their cultural lenses and the ideological frameworks that best match their beliefs. Typically, history students are asked to read other people's narratives, rather than create their own narratives, of the past. Instead, the history classroom should offer regular opportunities for students to conduct their own historical research. Rather than simply remember others' narratives, it would allow them to do their own intellectual lifting. It would ask that they consider other peoples' narratives, but within their own ideological frameworks and cultural perspectives. Moreover, this would give students a chance to construct important counter-narratives to those of mainstream history, which would be rooted in their own race, gender, class, and sexual identities (Paris & Alim, 2017).

When students learn to write their own interpretations and narratives, they are educated in a process that is similar to the types of analysis based on evidence that we need to perform as citizens. Much like historical evidence, civic evidence is often incomplete. In history, some records may have not survived, were never documented, or were intentionally destroyed. In the political world, evidence often suffers from the very same problems.

Often citizens must make judgments based on incomplete evidence, missing evidence, or evidence that may have been hidden (or destroyed). For example, in the early 2000s, as history teachers, we had to help students search and judge the evidence we had, and the students had to make their own decisions around their support or opposition to the Afghanistan and Iraq Wars. As more evidence became available, many of our students shifted in their views of the wars. Some began constructing their own counter-narratives to those of the mainstream media and Congress (which both had clear pro-war narratives). Certainly, not all students opposed the war. Some, especially those working from conservative or neoconservative frameworks, were more convinced war was necessary. Yet we feel that we provided an important thinking process for our students—one that they hopefully will continue to use as citizens to make sense of political events and issues.

When students learn how to create and change narratives using evidence, they are exercising a fundamental skill of activists, or what Moyer and colleagues (2001) called cultural preparation. In cultural preparation, activists must first recognize how their current society is different from the one they envision; they then must begin to reimagine how society would look if it was built on different principles. In their collective action, the activists must then understand and rewrite narratives to help convince the public that change is necessary. For example, before the modern civil rights movement, most White Americans believed racial segregation was warranted. The activists of the movement understood that they first needed to imagine a different world, and then to understand the narratives White people learned (and told) that validated the status quo. Finally, they needed to rewrite the narrative, offering counter-narratives of a society that was rebuilt on civil rights and fairness. These same skills should be learned by students, as they are asked to interpret the past based on their ideological frameworks and the historical evidence that we have at hand.

Presentism. If teachers are to help students develop as democratic citizens, they should help students see how the past was different than the present, but they should place more emphasis on helping the students use their present conceptions of justice to interpret the past. Numerous history educators (often working from a cognitive psychology perspective) have warned that teachers must avoid presentism in students' thinking (Lowenthal, 2000; Seixas & Morton, 2013; Wineburg, 1999, 2001). Wineburg (2001), using Lowenthal's analogy that the past is a foreign country, has defined presentism as "the act of viewing the past through the lens of the present" (p. 19). However, we would like to caution any oversimplification of this idea. Based on this concept, some teachers have told their students to not judge the past by present standards. However, this can become a slippery slope. In some cases, teachers may ask students to justify slavery, the removal of Indigenous people from their lands, or the incarceration of

Japanese Americans during World War II. Instead, as Barton and Levstik (2004) argued, we must ask students to make moral judgments about the past when studying history. As Lévesque (2008) has reminded us, this would also better align with the work of historians, as they contextualize the past within the present. He wrote,

> Because historians' interpretations are contextually situated in the present, these necessarily involve contemporary judgments on the meaning and signifi-cance of the selected past actions and actors . . . [they do not] simply investigate facts and leave moral judgments to others, but must perforce often make moral judgments themselves. (p. 153)

In fact, the idea of avoiding presentism has been debated at length since Carl Becker coined the term in 1912, when he used it to argue in favor of a study of history that is relevant to the present (Becker, 1932; Klein, 1985; Schonberger, 1974; Zinn, 1990). In this same argument, he explained that historians could not avoid their worldviews that guide their work (some-thing he learned from his advisor Frederick Jackson Turner; Klein, 1985). This was part of the foundation for his later argument, for which he became widely known, that every person can be their own historian and interpreter of the past (Becker, 1932; Klein, 1985).

We agree with Becker's conception of presentism, and we consider it to be a goal of historical study (while also carefully considering how the worldviews, perspectives, language, and cultures of people from the past were different from our own). Historians, history students, and citizens live in a period of the future, which has been the direct result of past actions. It is impossible for them to divorce their present-day perspectives from their interpretation of the past; otherwise, people in the present would be unable to reject past mistakes (e.g., slavery, colonization of Indigenous peoples, the Holocaust). Otherwise, we render historical study meaningless. It is crucial that students learn how people in the past thought, acted, and lived differ-ently than in the present. However, the historical record, problematically, may never allow us to fully understand all groups' experiences or thoughts (especially those groups that have been intentionally left out or erased from the record). Focusing on historical study as mainly a study of primary sources and how people thought in the past does not help us understand how those past events led to our present condition. Moreover, if teachers are overly focused on presentism, they may also be inhibiting students' abilities to de-velop activist thinking. If students are taught that people in the past must primarily be judged by past standards, they may also be taught that those who envisioned a new society with different structures were improper; it sends the message that most people thought a certain way, rendering it nor-mal and their beliefs appropriate. Instead, thinking like an activist helps stu-dents understand that certain groups working for justice, while sometimes ahead of their time, were envisioning a new, better society (see the "Cultural Preparation" section in Chapter 2) and creating a movement to challenge the status quo.

The point is not to teach students to avoid presentism. Rather, it is to help them understand the concept of presentism, so they can be more careful in how they interpret the past today. If the purpose of studying history is to develop a sense of the past to inform citizenship in the present (and future), then students must develop an understanding of how politics influences how history is written and rewritten. Rather than focusing heavily on having students avoid presentism, we argue that the history classroom should involve students continually being asked if people were treated fairly or justly during past events.

TRANSFORMATIVE DEMOCRATIC CITIZENSHIP IN ACTION

To examine what transformative democratic citizenship looks like in action, we will describe a school year in a racially diverse 8th-grade classroom in Austin, Texas. While the teacher, Ms. Ana Sanchez, will model transformative democratic citizenship in action, her classroom also embodies the concepts of critical multiculturalism, social inquiry, and thinking like an activist, which were addressed in previous chapters. It should be noted that Ms. Sanchez is based on one of the author's participants in a previous teaching study, and, while the events that follow are a synopsis of those that occurred in an actual classroom, some details have been modified.

Ms. Sanchez's story begins shortly after August 9, 2014, when Michael Brown, a Black teenager, was shot to death in Ferguson, Missouri, by a White police officer. A couple of weeks later, Ms. Sanchez's students came to her classroom on the first day of school upset about what had happened in Ferguson. They asked her right away, "Have you heard about Ferguson? Did you know that they shot Michael Brown while he had his hands in the air?" They wanted to discuss this issue and other instances of racism in their own community. Ms. Sanchez decided she needed to make space to discuss this in her classroom. Instead of reviewing the course syllabus and talking about class procedures, she restructured her first class to listen to the students. She had the students make a list of "things they have heard about Michael Brown and Ferguson," and then they used valid sources on the Internet to see what they could confirm. She then created a space where students could share their own reactions to this event, as well as share their own experiences with racial profiling and police brutality. She learned that her new group of 8th-graders had many experiences where they felt victimized by authority figures because of their race (which was not surprising, as she had heard numerous similar stories throughout her years in the classroom). Since the classroom was primarily comprised of students of color, she felt it was important that they could mourn Michael Brown, but also share their stories. In the last few minutes of class, she asked the students to journal. This helped them begin to process the event and their own experiences with racism. However, she knew she had much more work to do.

Over the next few weeks, Ms. Sanchez asked her students to create a new vision for society. She wrote the following question on the board: "If we could rebuild our society, what would it look like?" The students' responses varied. Their initial response was a world where Black and Brown kids (and adults) felt safe and people could give each other what they needed. As Ms. Sanchez continued to probe, her class spoke of a community without guns and with police they could trust (and more police who looked like them; 70% of Austin's police force was White). Slowly, the students moved away from a singular focus, such as the police or gun control, to examine more structural problems, such as poverty, education, and health care. The class started to analyze the systematic causes of inequality, such as unemployment, inequity in the prison system, lack of opportunity in schooling, and poverty. The students realized that to create a society where people of color feel safe, there must be equal opportunity. They envisioned a society where everyone had equal access to high-quality schools, Black men were as likely to get jobs as White men, and the police and community were partners, not adversaries. Ms. Sanchez's students were participating in cultural preparation, which is creating a new vision for society beyond the status quo. They also began to take part in critical analyses of oppression in the power structures.

To solidify the students' critical analyses, Ms. Sanchez created a curriculum that specifically examined oppression in power structures. She reorganized her course around the histories of Black and Brown communities in Texas and across the United States. She took the next 2 months to highlight some of the most important events leading up to the shooting of Michael Brown. She included historical examples of racial profiling and police brutality (including the LA Riots, Watts and Newark in the mid-1960s, the Zoot Suit and Detroit Race Riots during World War II, and the creation of exclusively White police forces in the 19th century), as well as their resistance by Black and Brown communities. She asked her students to take a critical eye at the past and to understand that there is a long history attached to what happened to Michael Brown. She also taught about how activists and movements banded together to protest and resist police brutality (including the actions of the Black Panther Party in the late 1960s).

After a critical look at the past, her students were ready to take part in collective action. If they had begun with collective action before taking part in cultural preparation (i.e., creating a new vision) and critical analysis (i.e., examining historical oppression in power structures), they would not have been as prepared to take part in collective action, and their work would not have been as meaningful. Ms. Sanchez assigned them a project for which they researched the historical roots of a social movement. She encouraged them to choose a movement related to racial justice or other social injustices. The students chose to research social movements related to undocumented immigrants, LGBTQ rights, Asian American rights, the women's liberation and the #MeToo movements, and climate change. Others opted to study the Black Lives Matter movement, Chicano student movement, and labor activism. First, the students analyzed the movement in the past, the methods the movement used, and if there had been any resultant social changes. They then wrote a brief memo to their classmates outlining what they found. Next, they were asked to analyze the tactics the movement used to create social change. They documented the methods that were used and how the groups worked within and against the system.

Ms. Sanchez also asked her students to consider what levels of government their social movements used to seek change (i.e., local, state, national, global). She then took them on a field trip to their statehouse (conveniently located in their hometown of Austin). During the field trip, students spoke with state legislators and their staffs about bills that they wanted to propose and how that linked to the specific social movements that they had studied. The students prepared specific questions and talking points related to those potential bills. Each group of students shared information about the related social movement from the past that they were studying, but they also asked questions about the current laws and policies in the state.

After the field trip, the students began the final phase of their social movement project. They were asked to choose what they thought was the most effective tactic(s) to bring about social change for their movement. Each group presented a revised memo about the history of their movement and the tactics used, and then they shared the tactical measures that were considered to be the most successful for enacting change today. The class then voted on the movement that they found to be most compelling. Using a set of criteria that they created, the students also voted on the tactic(s) that they believed would be most impactful for creating change. This was when the students went from conceptualizing movements to building movements.

The class decided that the Black Lives Matter movement was the most pressing issue, and they argued that a student walkout would be the most effective form of protest, which they connected to the walkouts of San Antonio and Crystal City, Texas (as well as East LA in California) in the late 1960s. In addition, the class decided to include other civic methods, such as a social media campaign bringing awareness using #BlackLivesMatter, a letter-writing campaign to their state and local officials calling for increased laws and policies related to community policing and police brutality, and a boycott of places that sell firearms (such as Walmart and Dick's Sporting Goods). Afterward, some students asked Ms. Sanchez if they could actually do their walkout. They told her that University of Texas students were organizing a walkout next week and that they wanted to join. Ms. Sanchez was not sure if her school administrators would support that. She was in a conundrum; here she was advocating for civic action, but she also did not want her students (or herself) to face any sort of punishment for engaging in civic action. She did also realize that civil disobedience only works if it involves public consequences. She acknowledged that classrooms are usually only spaces to simulate democracy; they are not actually places to *do* democracy. She wanted to change that.

The students told Ms. Sanchez that they would protest with or without her (she had prepared them well). As they began work on their walkout, Ms. Sanchez told them they needed approval from their principal (she also wanted to be mindful of their own academic success). At first the students were not happy; they explained to Ms. Sanchez that they had done all this work, and if the protest was not approved it would be unfair. She helped them brainstorm what could be done if the principal said no. They discussed having the protests during nonschool hours or off school grounds, and they discussed asking community members and leaders to help with the protest. The students worked on their presentation to the school's principal with the hope of her approval.

The students' completed presentation detailed the history of the Black Lives Matter movement and police brutality. They created empathy by including the voices of students from their school (some drawn from the first week of the semester, when students journaled about personal experiences). They laid out a detailed plan for the walkout, including addressing issues of safety, since the school is near some high-traffic streets. After hearing the presentation, the principal agreed to allow the students to have the Black Lives Matter walkout. She also volunteered to include key community members and to inform members of the press.

On the morning of the day of the walkout, the students were filled with energy. They had been working for several classes to prepare a press release, speeches, chants, and signs. Ms. Sanchez cannot remember her students ever feeling this empowered and invested in their work. They had previously passed out fliers and announced over the school PA system their mission:

> We, the students and the staff of this middle school, are planning a demonstration to support and increase awareness that Black Lives Matter, inspired by the deaths of Michael Brown and so many more. We need not only the voices of our youth but the support of the adults to protest against the unjust police brutality, inequality, and racial profiling taking place across the nation, as well as right here in our community. We not only want the support from YOU but the support from your family, too. These injustices based on race have been happening our whole lives.

The entire student body of the school walked out, as well as the principal and some teachers. The majority of the protestors were dressed in all black. Ms. Sanchez journaled about the experience:

> We all walked out of the building together. We gave two bullhorns to the students and they started chanting. . . . There was a lot of traffic and the signs were big enough for the cars to read. The students got a lot of honking in support. We were outside from about 8:00–9:30 a.m. At some points the students were standing on the side of the road and at other points the students were marching in a circle. Before we started walking back to the school, I took the bullhorn and reminded the students that they had just been a part of making history. I told them Ferguson would one day be in the history books and now they could say they had participated in that struggle against police brutality. We returned to the auditorium at around 9:45 a.m. The school librarian was waiting for us in the auditorium. She is an older Black woman who has been at the school for several years. She ended up taking charge of the debrief. She told the students she was very proud of them but had one important question: "Why did you do it?" The tone of the room seemed quiet and reflective. Students started slowly raising their hands to answer. We spent about 45 minutes debriefing in this way. Students started raising their hands and sharing their personal reasons for joining the protest. Adults (I think there were about 10 adults in the room by this point) started telling the students why they were proud of them. Then the two Black teachers, who are also young (in their 20s), shared their stories of being racially profiled by police. This prompted students to start sharing their stories about the police or about feeling discriminated against that we had talked about back in September. The students now had a larger audience to share. Some students and adults were crying. It was a very powerful experience to be part of.

The students referenced their protest in class throughout the remainder of the year.

Days after the march, the students were impressed to see their names and faces in the local newspaper. The press mainly applauded them. However, one student brought in comments from the online version of the news story, where an anonymous person called the kids un-American and said that Ms. Sanchez had wasted a whole year of the students' lives by teaching them to be "Democrat activists." Another anonymous comment said that 8th-graders do not have the intelligence yet to make decisions on issues like these and they had no right to tell law enforcement officials when not to use firearms. Some of the students were upset and saddened by the online comments. Ms. Sanchez used these comments as a teachable moment and explained that every movement has to confront setbacks and people who resist social change. She asked the students to reflect on the movements they researched and to think of all the hardships and resistance that those groups faced. She asked each student to come back to class the next day and share a story from their social movement of how it dealt with opposition and resistance. The exercise helped students see that part of social change and activism is dealing with resistance and opposition to the goals and people of the movement. The students seemed to gain a greater empathy for the work of social activism. Many of them said they were going to continue to protest, especially for the social issue from their class project.

Ms. Sanchez's lessons about movements and social change continued throughout the remainder of the year. In the spring, she asked the students to journal about their experiences during the past year in their history classroom. She asked if they had changed and, if so, how. Many of the students described being transformed by this classroom experience; they felt that they had the power to enact change. Others reported that this was the first time that they cared about learning history, especially because it helped them in the current world. The students discussed how it made them want to vote regularly and attend protests for issues that they cared about. They were empowered, and they described themselves as activists who had the power to change the future. This was transformative democratic citizenship in action.

CHAPTER 6

U.S. History at the High School Level
Ms. María Lopez

In the previous chapters, we discussed the importance of helping students develop their "thinking like an activist" skills in relation to historical events (see Chapter 2), and we outlined three main pedagogical concepts related to teaching history for justice: social inquiry (see Chapter 3), critical multiculturalism (see Chapter 4), and transformative democratic citizenship (see Chapter 5). We have discussed how these ideas are rooted in theory and are supported by research inside and outside history education. We also argued that the main purpose of history education, which we referred to as teaching history for justice, must be for students to understand how the concept of inequity developed over time, how it functioned in the past (which has led to the present), and how movements of people have organized to create more just societies.

In this next section of the book, we attempt to bridge the theory and research on teaching history for justice with classroom practice. In 1995, Gloria Ladson-Billings called for more models of culturally relevant teaching to help support teachers by providing examples of doing this work (Gladson-Billings, 1995a). More recently, Chris Emdin (2011) argued that it is essential to also "provide teachers with tangible tools that support them in becoming transformative pedagogues" (p. 286). We acknowledge that without examples of how this pedagogy is implemented in the classroom, history for justice is likely to have less influence on teachers' practices. Toward those ends, we use the work of Joyce and colleagues (2004) and their models of teaching to create several vignettes of teachers' practices, which we offer as illustrations for how this work can be enacted in the history classroom.

In the following chapters, we describe four vignettes based on real history teachers' practices to inspire other teachers to do this justice-oriented work. The vignettes focus on the following imagined teachers: Ms. María Lopez (high school–level U.S. history; this chapter), Mr. Tom Kulig (high school–level world history; see Chapter 7), Ms. Joyce Smith (middle school–level ancient world history; see Chapter 8), and Mr. Frank Hashimoto (elementary school–level state and local history; see Chapter 9). While the teachers are imagined, they are an amalgamation of practices that we have learned from the numerous teachers we have had the privilege of researching over the past decade. Most of the practices in the vignettes come directly from the teachers who were observed or interviewed during our numerous studies of history classrooms (Martell, 2013, 2015, 2016, 2017, 2018; Martell & Stevens, 2017a, 2017b; Stevens & Martell, 2016, 2019), or they were practices that we used ourselves as classroom teachers. We also intentionally present teachers from different backgrounds, grade levels, and geographic locations and communities to highlight how this work can be done in different places. Each chapter describes one of the teacher's classrooms and includes descriptions of their classroom culture, pedagogical approaches, curriculum, and assessments over a school year.

We hope that these vignettes help us reenvision what the history classroom could and should look like. In the tradition of the many other critical race, feminist, and queer scholars in our field, we hope these vignettes offer counter-narratives and revisionist histories that speak back to power and dominant narratives in both history and education (Delgado & Stefancic, 2012; King & Chandler, 2016; Ladson-Billings & Tate, 1995). They might offer a classroom counter-story, which provides ways to transform history classrooms that have traditionally been dominated by White, male, straight, middle-class, and wealthy narratives into justice-oriented classrooms that help students understand how inequity has been created and maintained.

HISTORY FOR JUSTICE IN THE U.S. HISTORY CLASSROOM

As we discussed in previous chapters, the main idea underlying history for justice is teaching students to think like an activist and examine movements for change across history. Inside the classroom, we contend that students should have opportunities to practice activism and learn how they can use democratic levers of change. Through engaging in informed action, students become more comfortable being advocates, and it can empower them to participate in activism outside the classroom.

Another important component of history for justice is its ability to show students that social change is more likely to occur through movements. Rarely have changes in human history been driven by individuals; instead, changes are usually driven by movements of people working for justice, and often through long-term and sustained efforts. For example, the modern civil rights movement did not begin in 1954 with *Brown v. Board of Education* (as many textbooks portray); it began almost 200 years earlier with the first abolitionists and extended through the Civil War and Reconstruction (where a legal framework was conceived by groups like the National Association for the Advancement of Colored People, which laid the groundwork for several civil rights movements), and it continues today (through movements like Black Lives Matter). This chapter illustrates how high school teachers can help high school students analyze the past within a U.S. history course. We start at the beginning of the school year and follow the teacher and their students until the end of the school year.

MS. MARÍA LOPEZ'S HIGH SCHOOL U.S. HISTORY CLASSROOM

Ms. María Lopez grew up in the Roxbury neighborhood of Boston and attended the city's public school system from kindergarten through high school. Her grandparents were migrants from Puerto Rico, and she was raised in a deeply connected Puerto Rican diaspora community. After high school, she attended a traditional undergraduate teacher preparation program at a large public university in Massachusetts and later earned a master's degree in education. She was a student teacher at a predominantly Black and Latinx public high school in Boston, where she taught U.S. history. After graduating, she was hired at the same school. Ms. Lopez is now in her sixth year as a teacher and teaches primarily U.S. history to 10th-grade students. She is also the advisor to the school's Latina affinity group and dance team.

Classroom Culture

Before the school year begins, Ms. Lopez is thinking about building a strong culture in her classroom. She is envisioning what her classroom community will look like. After reading Gloria Ladson-Billings's (2009) *The Dreamkeepers* during her teacher preparation program, she fell in love with the idea that a classroom should feel like a family. She wants to get to know each of her students as soon as she can and considers them as her nieces and nephews. She deeply cares about their success, even when they may struggle or need emotional support. On the first day of school, she asks students to introduce themselves by sharing one way that they or their families were a part of history. Some students say they attended Barack Obama's inauguration, others describe ancestors who were Wampanoag people (the first nation of their area) or were on the Mayflower (the settlers who later occupied the land), and still others describe their parents' or grandparents' immigration stories. Many students say that they have struggled with history class, and Ms. Lopez tells them that her goal this year is to help them connect to history and learn how their ancestors were part of the larger story of the past.

Since Ms. Lopez's class focuses on justice, she tells the students that sometimes discussions might get difficult in class, perhaps even emotional. She explains that when they are discussing an issue and students disagree or a topic may make them upset, it is important that they support each other. During the first week of school, Ms. Lopez asks her students to create guidelines for the classroom to help them be supportive of each other during difficult talks throughout the school year:

1. It is important to listen first, think second, and speak third.
2. Consider other ideas. You do not have to agree, but you should at least try to understand why someone has a different view or perspective from you.
3. We can challenge ideas and arguments, not individuals. Avoid making it personal (you, them) and instead challenge the idea or the argument (it).
4. You don't represent a group; you only represent yourself. You should never be asked to speak for others.
5. You can always step out of the room if a conversation makes you uncomfortable, anxious, or any other emotion that may do you harm.

As a teacher, Ms. Lopez starts with the assumption that her students mean well, and she shares with them that each day "we reset"; she does not remind students of negative past experiences. When situations may become difficult with a student, she listens first and tries to understand the student's perspective (which reflects her classroom guidelines).

Ms. Lopez spends the first few weeks of the school year building her class culture. Her room is decorated with student work for all to admire, and students self-select what work to post around the room. She does not place the desks in rows, but in a U-shape to foster conversation. There is a student quote board, where interesting and insightful comments from class are displayed. Ms. Lopez also intentionally chooses to display images and documents on the walls that are representative of the many different voices of the past; she wants students to see their racial, gender, class, and sexual orientation identities represented. For one of the first class assignments, she asks the students to bring in a paper bag that includes five items that they consider part of their histories (including their families' histories). Next, they conduct a "show and tell" and share about themselves. The students' first homework assignment is called the "My History Project," where they are asked to write about how they and their families connect to history. Ms. Lopez reads the students' papers and comments throughout the papers, thanking them for sharing and finding commonalties. While reading these papers, she keeps a running list of the students' social identities, beliefs, and interests to build into her classroom's curriculum. Ms. Lopez also photocopies these papers and keeps a copy, so she can reread them when planning.

Ms. Lopez's family approach to the classroom continues throughout the year. After greeting her students at the door, she sometimes spends the first 5 or 10 minutes of class encouraging them to ask questions about events they saw in the news, especially events that relate to their cultures or communities. This student inquiry of the news encourages them to be critical readers of current events, but it also creates a classroom that regularly asks them to connect the past to the present. During the independent work, Ms. Lopez conducts frequent "check-ins" with individual students about their academic work, as well as about their personal well-being. At the end of each semester, students set goals for their own growth and academic progress; midway through the semester, she holds conferences with the students about their progress toward those goals. Four times a year, Ms. Lopez's students participate in open circle, where they honor fellow classmates and share what they have recently learned from each other. It is an important moment for them to highlight what they appreciate about each other and how they have helped each other grow.

Pedagogical Approaches

While Ms. Lopez uses many different pedagogical techniques in her classroom, her pedagogy is most aligned with what Martell (2018) described as *challenging*, "where a teacher views the role as helping students develop different analytical lenses for questioning the world around them" (p. 71). Her main goal is to help "students recognize injustice, while ultimately encouraging them to become agents of change" (Martell & Stevens, 2019, p. 4). She often asks her students to use sociological lenses when examining the past. She values inquiry-based instruction and routinely has the students answer historical questions using evidence. However, she is not the only person in her classroom asking the questions. Early in the school year, her students practice asking their own historical questions and become acquainted with different source repositories, so they will eventually take the lead on the historical inquiries. She guides her students to see that sources from well-known figures from the past are not more valuable than those from everyday people. She encourages them to see how historians use primary, secondary, and tertiary sources to craft their narratives, and that one type of source is not inherently more reliable than another. Instead, as a historian or citizen should, she has her students use all three types of sources together, while gauging their reliability, when making judgments about the past. For Ms. Lopez, inquiry is a process for analyzing historical events using different social lenses (race, class, gender, etc.) with the intention of developing empathy and challenging students' preconceived notions of the past.

During the year, Ms. Lopez continues to foster a family approach to the classroom using different pedagogical techniques. She reminds herself that learning is a process and intelligence is not fixed. She deeply believes that everyone, including herself and her students, can improve. At the same time, she is very aware of the criticisms of the "growth mindset" work in education, and she recently shared with her colleagues a story from the HuffPost on Luke Wood's criticism of it (Hilton, 2017), where he argued that it is an incomplete idea, often misused by White teachers to avoid praising Black students and other students of color for their academic abilities, talent, or intellect. She agrees, believing it is important to affirm not only students' efforts but also their abilities, especially for students of color. It leads to a powerful conversation during a department meeting about how the history teachers could better support the intellectual and academic development of their students, especially their Black and Brown students.

Ms. Lopez explains to her students that learning should be student-centered and that their voices need to be heard within her classroom. She implements several strategies with them so they can share their thinking both orally and in writing. Many strategies are designed to help raise the voice of students who do not usually participate in whole-class discussion. For example, during one class, she has the students analyze primary sources related to Reconstruction. She hangs chart paper around the room with questions and primary sources, and the students write their reactions to each, as well as respond to the reactions of their classmates. She grounds these silent conversations with essential questions related to systematic in-equity, and she asks her students to challenge the status quo. For instance, one source related to the lynching of Black people in the period after the Civil War causes the students to have a thoughtful, yet emotional, response. One student, who rarely speaks in class, wrote, "I don't know how anyone can argue that Black people were free after the Civil War, when they were constantly being terrorized by White mobs. The fear of that alone would prevent anyone from speaking out or protesting!" During the whole-class discussion, Ms. Lopez highlights this comment and has the class dig deeper into the role of racism and violence after the Civil War.

Curriculum

Ms. Lopez finds strategic ways to use the content of the state-mandated history curriculum to teach history for justice. While she covers the main topics listed, she also realizes that the curriculum does not describe how those lists of names, dates, and places should be taught. As a result, Ms. Lopez decides to organize her U.S. history course around the following essential questions: What is freedom? Throughout U.S. history, who has had freedom and who has not? How did certain movements successfully expand freedom for all?

Unit 1: Indigenous People: The First Nations. Ms. Lopez's curriculum begins with a unit on the Indigenous peoples who first lived in the Americas. As part of that unit, she begins with a mini-unit on Indigenous societies before European colonization, which starts with a lesson where students use archaeological evidence to debate about how the first people came to the Americas. Next, her lessons focus on the different groups of Indigenous people across North and South America, with a specific focus on the Mexica (Aztecs),

Mayans, Incas, Mississippian, and Algonquin peoples. Finally, once they have a strong understanding of the Native peoples, students learn about the Arawak and Taíno peoples' first interactions with Christopher Columbus from their perspective, which is followed by the conflicts caused by other European groups invading and settling on Native land. This is particularly important for many of Ms. Lopez's students, because like her family, they or their ancestors came from islands in the Caribbean, like Puerto Rico, the Dominican Republic, and Haïti. During one of the first lessons on the European invasion, the class uses the Zinn Education Project's Columbus lesson plan, where they use historical evidence to answer the question: Who is responsible for the death of millions of Taínos on the island of Hispaniola in the late 15th century? They examine numerous people and groups, including Columbus, Columbus's men, the king and queen, the Taínos, and the system of empire. Students are asked to defend each group in a debate. This activity leads to a passionate discussion about who was responsible, and ultimately students come away with a more complex understanding of how such destruction of Native societies could have occurred.

At the end of the unit, Ms. Lopez highlights two movements for change during this period: Arawak resistance to Columbus and the "Protectors of the Indians" (primarily missionaries, like Bartolomé de las Casas, who attempted to stop the brutality of European conquest). She chose these two groups to juxtapose two very different change movements. The first movement was led by oppressed people, while the second was led by people from within the oppressor group. Both groups were needed to dismantle systems of oppression; however, Ms. Lopez also highlights that both groups engaged in justice work for different reasons. The Arawak's movement was one of self-defense and cultural protection. The "Protectors of the Indians" were guided by their desire to Christianize and "save souls." Ms. Lopez also uses this as an opportunity to show the shortcomings of certain groups (especially in this case, the shortcomings of the missionaries, who were working within settler-colonizer frameworks), while also highlighting the concept of interest convergence (the theory that advances for oppressed groups will be pursued when they converge with the interests and ideologies of the dominant groups).

Unit 2: White Settlers and Indigenous Resistance. While U.S. history teachers traditionally organize their European colonization units around White conquistadors, Ms. Lopez instead organizes her unit around Indigenous resistance. She focuses on various Indigenous groups and the ways that they defended their cultures and societies. Since many of her students are Latinx, she attempts to show the experiences of different Native groups in the Americas that faced both similar and different challenges as a result of the European invasion. This unit includes several lessons comparing the experiences of the Aztecs and the Incas to help students see two very different reactions to European colonization. Students read excerpts from Eduardo Galeano's (1997) *Open Veins of Latin America*, which examines the so-called "discovery" of the "New World" from Indigenous and Latin American perspectives. The unit ends with students presenting the stories of colonization from the Indigenous perspective, including the Taíno, the Aztecs, the Incas, the Tupi, the Powhatan, the Wampanoag, and the Mi'kmaq.

Unit 3: The American Revolution. In her unit on the American Revolution, instead of highlighting a few important leaders of the Revolution (i.e., Samuel Adams, John Hancock, Paul Revere, Thomas Jefferson, George Washington), Ms. Lopez teaches it as a collective movement of people. Moreover, she highlights that both the patriots and the loyalists were diverse coalitions (including Black, Native, and White people, people from different social classes, and women and men), and she examines why different members of each group would have sided with one group over the other (often splitting communities). For example, she uses a lesson where students write diaries about the key events of the American Revolution from the perspectives of a diverse group of people, including Prince Hall (Black patriot), Colonel Tye/Titus Cornelius (Black loyalist), Fortune Burnee Jr. (Native patriot), Thayendanegea/Joseph Brant (Native loyalist), Phyllis Wheatley (Black patriot), Deborah Sampson (White patriot), Samuel Adams (White patriot), and Benedict Arnold (White patriot turned loyalist).

Unit 4: The Constitution and Early Republic. In her unit on the Constitution and Early Republic, Ms. Lopez uses an overarching question: Who was the new Constitution written for? In this unit, students examine primary sources from the Constitutional Convention, considering how the framers debated the issues of race (i.e., Indigenous sovereignty, slavery) but were also silent on the rights of women. The students also read one of the strongest rebuttals to the Constitution from Mercy Otis Warren, who secretly wrote an anti-federalist pamphlet under a pseudonym that intentionally hid her gender.

Unit 5: Expansion or Invasion? Instead of calling her next unit Westward Expansion, which embeds a view that White Americans had a right to move west, Ms. Lopez asks students to consider if it was an "expansion" or an "invasion." She asks them to examine the question: How should we remember the expansion of the United States in the first half of the 19th century? This unit starts with lessons on Sacagawea's role in helping the Lewis and Clark Expedition and ends with a lesson on the California Gold Rush and the Compromise of 1850. Ms. Lopez uses a documentary that highlights the important role that Sacagawea played in the group's survival. During this unit, Ms. Lopez uses visual thinking strategies to have students examine John Gast's 1872 painting titled *Manifest Destiny*. They are amazed by the depiction of Indigenous people in the darkness running away from the so-called "angel of progress." One student tells her that "this is pretty racist" and interprets the painting as a clear message that White people were taking over the land to make their nation.

Unit 6: Abolition. Unlike what is taught through the traditional U.S. history curriculum, Ms. Lopez chooses to teach abolition, Civil War, and Reconstruction as one larger unit. She says it is important to show that the Civil War led to the abolition of slavery, but it is as important to know what happened before and after the war that led to a further entrenchment of racial oppression for African Africans. Ms. Lopez frames student learning around the following questions: How could race-based oppression (i.e., slavery, segregation, assimilation policies) have lasted so long in the United States? Why were the Civil War and Reconstruction unsuccessful in creating racial and gender equity? While the war itself is important, much of Ms. Lopez's unit focuses on the social changes that occurred and did not occur before, during, and after the Civil War. She believes that studying Reconstruction is possibly more important than studying the Civil War, because it ingrained systems of oppression and segregation into the government that would last to the current day. One of the last lessons in this unit involves a debate about which civil rights leader had the best plan for Black liberation: Booker T. Washington, W. E. B. Du Bois, or Marcus Garvey. Most of the students feel that Du Bois's and Garvey's ideas were the best, but they feel that Washington's ideas may have had more of an impact on American society. At the end of the unit, Ms. Lopez assigns students to various justice movements from each period (i.e., abolition, Civil War, Reconstruction, early Jim Crow era), and she asks them to analyze if those movements were successful and to present their analysis to the class. For example, one group is assigned the anti-lynching movement of the early 20th century. Since several of the students are involved in the school's drama club, they decide to compose a play based on the life of Ida B. Wells and how she organized a movement against lynching.

Unit 7: Immigration and Industrialization. Ms. Lopez centers her unit on immigration and industrialism around her students and their families' American experiences. To do this, she starts the unit by having her students engage in critical family histories. They use publicly available digital government documents (e.g., census records, immigration documents, slavery records) to examine their own families' histories. She asks the students to consider ways that their families' experiences involved privilege and disadvantage. For instance, one student named Crismely investigated her ancestors' immigration from the Dominican Republic. Using databases of U.S. immigration and baptism records, she was able to trace her family's history back four generations in the Dominican Republic and then trace her great grandfather's journey through Ellis Island and his settlement in New York City. She was also able to trace her grandparents' move from New York to Boston. To connect her family's experience to the larger Dominican immigration story, she read several books about Dominican American history. To build on what she learned, she interviewed her grandmother and mother about their family's histories. Her report paints a complex story of her family's journey—one that showed moments of opportunity, but also how inequity impacted them. Ms. Lopez has the students present their critical family histories to the class and then asks them to brainstorm the similarities and differences of their families' histories.

After the students have a chance to examine their own histories through a critical lens, they then start to study immigration at the turn of the 20th century. Unlike what is presented in the traditional U.S. history curriculum, Ms. Lopez intentionally presents immigration during this period as being global (not only European). In one of the first lessons, she has students examine immigration records from East and South Asians at Angel Island; Mexican immigrants at Eagle Pass, Texas; Caribbean and South Americans at Ellis Island, New York; and French Canadians at St. Albans, Vermont. While students examine several historical sources showing that Europeans were the largest group of immigrants during this period, she asks them to consider the effect on immigrants of color being much smaller populations and how that affected immigration policy. She also has students read excerpts from Matthew Frye Jacobson's *Whiteness of a Different Color: European Immigrants and the Alchemy of Race*, which examines the racial hierarchy of Whiteness in the United States at this time. Several students, especially White students, are fascinated to learn that while White immigrants held certain privileges compared to immigrants of color, White immigrants from certain places (i.e., Southern Europe, Eastern Europe, French Canada) were not considered fully White. Ms. Lopez also uses this lesson to discuss the complexities of colorism and the race-based system of discrimination both within and against Latinx communities during this time. Toward the end of this unit, she also introduces the concepts of forced reservations and boarding schools for Indigenous people. She does this to show the relationships between the large influx of immigrants coming to the East Coast and the treatment of Native people in the West. At the same time, she highlights numerous acts of Indigenous resistance (e.g., Wounded Knee, Geronimo, the Ghost Dance movement) to show a more complex story of the so-called "closing of the frontier" (as the textbook describes it).

Ms. Lopez next shifts the unit to workers' rights. She covers the major strikes of the era, including the Haymarket Riot, Pullman Strike, Homestead Strike, and the Ludlow Massacre. She then uses the city of Chicago as a case study of immigrant and labor rights during the era. This involves showing a public broadcasting documentary on Chicago and having students engage in a mock trial of the Pullman strikers. The unit ends with a review of important Supreme Court cases from the era, where Ms. Lopez highlights both advances and setbacks for organized labor. At the end of the unit, the students must examine five key justice movements (and several of their key activists) from the era, and they must determine the most effective "level of change" that the movements used: workers' rights (Eugene V. Debs, Lucy Gonzales Parsons, Emma Goldman), anti-lynching (Ida B. Wells, Juanita Jackson Mitchell, Angelina Grimké), anti-segregation (W. E. B. Du Bois, William Monroe Trotter), and Native sovereignty (Sitting Bull, Geronimo).

Unit 8: World at War. Often the world wars are taught as separate units bookending the Roaring 20s and the Great Depression. However, Ms. Lopez teaches them as one unit to emphasize how their events were related. Since the students covered both of the world wars extensively in their previous world history course, Ms. Lopez also organizes this era around social movements (spending less time on battles or military strategy) and has students investigate the question: Did the world wars and the New Deal expand or reduce freedom for people in the United States? The unit emphasizes how different groups experienced the period. Ms. Lopez starts the unit with students examining several events and their relationship to civil liberties, including the Zimmerman Note, the sinking of the *Lusitania*, the Espionage and Sedition Acts, *Schenck v. United States*, racism against African American World War I soldiers, the imprisonment of Eugene V. Debs and Emma Goldman, and the Palmer Raids. The students are asked to make group presentations on the essential question, with many arguing that the period curtailed Americans' freedoms.

During the portion of the unit on the Roaring 20s and the Great Depression, Ms. Lopez assigns students to various historical figures from diverse racial, gender, and class backgrounds. She has them journal about the major events from the perspective of their assigned person; these events include the economic boom of the 1920s and the outcomes of the 1929 crash. This assignment allows students to consider how various groups experienced the boom and bust, and how the intersection of race, gender, and class had an impact on their experience.

The unit ends with an examination of World War II from different perspectives. Ms. Lopez assigns students to one of five groups: Japanese Americans, Mexican Americans, African Americans, Italian Americans, and Indigenous peoples. She asks the students to research their assigned group's experiences related to several major events in the war. As they read through primary and secondary sources, students are asked to respond based on the perspective of their assigned group. For example, when studying the Zoot Suit Riots in Los Angeles, the students are asked to describe how their group may have written a news article based on the event. The unit highlights five case studies from the war: Jewish refugees and the MS *St. Louis*, Japanese American incarceration, Zoot Suit Riots and the Bracero Program, the Detroit Race Riots and the Double-V Campaign, and the Navajo Code Talkers and Native resistance to the war. The unit ends with a discussion of the atomic bomb use on Japan, where students examine American and Japanese perspectives, including the anime film *Barefoot Gen*, the John Hersey book *Hiroshima*, and Langston Hughes's statements on the role of race in the decision to use the atomic bomb on the Japanese. One of Ms. Lopez's main goals is to show the role of racial solidarity during this era, but that people of color were often intentionally divided by White people in power to prevent collaboration against racism.

Unit 9: Mid-20th-Century Movements for Justice. Ms. Lopez combines the modern civil rights and anti-war movements into a larger unit on mid-20th-century justice movements. Her students finish the unit knowing that there was not one civil rights movement or one anti-war movement; instead, there were numerous movements involving conflicting opinions and ideas. Ms. Lopez also wants students to know that these movements did not represent the majority of Americans, and that justice movements are often working against a public opinion that favors the status quo. For instance, she begins the mini-unit on civil rights by asking: How many different views of the civil rights movements were there? The students then study various groups from the era, including: National Association for the Advancement of Colored People, Southern Christian Leadership Conference, Student Nonviolent Coordinating Committee, Nation of Islam, and Black Panther Party. Through the use of primary and secondary sources, she helps students see that some groups used a legal strategy, while others used a nonviolent resistance strategy, and yet others used any means necessary. She then follows a similar structure for the students' examinations of César Chávez, Dolores Huerta, and the United Farm Workers; José Angel Gutiérrez and the Mexican American Youth Organization; the East Los Angeles Walkouts; and the Young Lords. Additionally, she covers movements related to Indigenous and Asian American rights, including the Third World Liberation Front, the American Indian Movement, the Occupation of Alcatraz and Wounded Knee, the Peter Yew Police Brutality Protests, the 1982 New York Chinatown Garment Strike, and the murder of Vincent Chin.

Unit 10: The Current Era. Ms. Lopez's final unit is on the current historical era, where she asks students to take on the role of a historian focused on justice, like those they have studied, and write the history of the last 40 years. The students are allowed to use different mediums to display their analysis, including planning and painting a local mural, writing and performing a play or song, or writing a graphic novel to be shared with their peers. They study Reagan's social policies, the Gulf War, the Rodney King beating and the LA Riots, 1990s welfare reform, 9/11, the Afghanistan and Iraq Wars, Hurricane Katrina, the Great American Boycott/Day Without an Immigrant, the murder of Trayvon Martin, Occupy Wall Street, the Tea Party movement, the Black Lives Matter (BLM) movement, Standing Rock and the Water Protectors, the #MeToo movement, the Never Again movement, and other movements for justice. In this unit, she uses a significant amount of audio and video, not typically used in the history classroom, such as music videos, spoken word poetry, artwork, and clips of news footage of the events.

Field Experiences and Classroom Guests

Ms. Lopez knows that learning does not only occur through classroom activities. Therefore, she plans several opportunities for her students to experience history-related field trips outside the classroom, as well as interact with community members inside the classroom. At the beginning of the year, Ms. Lopez starts her unit on the American Revolution by taking her students on a field trip to Boston's Freedom Trail, where she highlights the important role that people of color, women, and the working classes played. They make stops at the African Meeting House and Abiel Smith School, which were the core religious and educational institutions of Boston's Black community after the American Revolution. When they reach the Granary Burying Ground, Ms. Lopez highlights the gravesite of Frank, an enslaved person owned by John Hancock, and the students discuss the complexity of someone fighting against tyranny while owning slaves. After learning about the Boston Massacre at its site, they walk to Faneuil Hall (Boston's first town hall), where they learn that a slave auction was once held next to the historical site. When they reach the North End, they learn about the Daughters of Liberty and the role that women played in the American Revolution. After hearing the story of Paul Revere's midnight ride at the Old North Church, they examine historical documents related to the church's Black freeman and women members. They end the field trip in the Copp's Hill Burying Ground, where they examine two conflicting historical figures buried there from Ibram X. Kendi's *Stamped from the Beginning*, White minister Cotton Mather (who was an importer of many racist and sexist ideas from Europe) and Black poet Phillis Wheatley (who defied many of Mather's racist and sexist ideas).

    After the field trip to Boston's Freedom Trail, Ms. Lopez has the students examine the life of Crispus Attucks through various sources, including an advertisement for a reward for his capture as a runaway slave, information on his African and Indigenous ancestry, and information on his life as a sailor. Students then engage in a mock trial of the Boston Massacre, where they must determine if the British soldiers are responsible for killing Attucks and the four other men. After the mock trial, Ms. Lopez has the students read an article from a local historian that describes how John Adams used a racist defense during the soldiers' trial, where he emphasized Attucks's race as a defense, telling the jury that he was "a stout Molatto fellow, whose very looks, was enough to terrify any person" (Minardi, 2010, p. 47). Students are shocked by this, as most had concluded that the British soldiers were guilty of murder (despite the reality that they were actually acquitted at the trial). Ms. Lopez uses an excerpt from another historian that shows that the lower social standings of the victims of the Boston Massacre may have also allowed the jury to be convinced that they were a violent group. Students were able to see how race and class may have played a major role in the verdict.

Before the holiday break, Ms. Lopez has her students participate in a series of activities where they challenge the status quo. For example, they participate in a "Day of Social Justice" where they are asked to live each minute of that day considering the advantages of social privilege and the ways to work against oppression. During this assignment, the students must consider institutional and personal forms of discrimination; they are asked to not only avoid obvious acts of bias and exclusion, but also consider ways to change the systems that govern their world. They keep a journal during the day, and they focus on how they use social media, the language they and their peers use, and their interactions with peers (such as who they sit with at lunch). After this activity, they are asked about how the systems of oppression that they noticed are passed down in their own families. They are asked to examine if these same behaviors and systems existed when their parents or grandparents were their age.

When the students reach the unit that includes World War II, Ms. Lopez invites a community member who was incarcerated in a Japanese American concentration camp to come speak with her students. The speaker describes her life before, during, and after "camp," and the students ask numerous prepared questions about what her experience was like, and how it informs her actions today. The guest speaker tells the students that it is the main reason she is involved in civil rights groups, like the Japanese American Citizens League (which became a civil rights organization after the war), and why she recently attended a protest at the U.S.–Mexico border related to the government's use of similar camps to detain refugees from Central America.

During her unit on the modern civil rights movement, Ms. Lopez takes her students on a field trip to historical sites related to civil rights in Boston. She explains that it is important for her to show how Boston was and still is part of the civil rights struggle, and that it was not always on the right side of history. This field trip starts with the John F. Kennedy Presidential Library, which portrays him as having a positive role in civil rights legislation, but Ms. Lopez also supplies several primary sources that show that he did not want to go further on civil rights, because he feared it would impact his reelection. Next, the students go downtown, where they are given a packet with images of different civil rights–related sites. At each site, Ms. Lopez has the students envision what it was like during the mid-20th century. These sites include the Boston Common Bandstand, where Martin Luther King Jr. led a march from the Roxbury neighborhood and led a rally of 22,000 people for more funding and integration of the public schools; City Hall Plaza, the site of an antibusing rally that led to Stanley Forman's photograph titled *The Soiling of Old Glory*; the South End, which is the historical gay community of Boston and where one of the first Pride Marches took place after the Stonewall Riots in New York City; and Chinatown to highlight Asian American activism in the 1970s and 1980s. They end the field trip by going to South Boston High School, which was the epicenter of the protests by White people against the desegregation of busing.

At the high school, outside, Ms. Lopez tells the history of the protests through a series of photographs from the time. Her students then proceed inside the building, where Ms. Lopez has organized a student-led symposium on race today in Boston with a colleague. The two Boston schools' students have created three panels. The first involves community policing and civil rights. The second relates to Asian and Latinx students' concerns (as the students felt they were often invisible when discussions of race occurred). The third is a space to discuss a series of race-related incidents in the Boston community. Ms. Lopez describes the importance of their field trip as it shows how the past connects to the present, and that there is still much more work to do toward justice.

Near the end of the school year, Ms. Lopez invites current leaders of the local chapter of BLM to discuss their activism related to issues of race and racism. Students have a chance to hear about how the local leaders drafted their platform and organized their public protests. Afterward, the students have many questions directly related to their activist work. At the end, the class breaks into several groups based on current issues of justice, and the local BLM activists act as "consultants," advising them on the most effective ways they could effect change. It is an incredibly powerful classroom activity. Ms. Lopez describes it as the moment she could see her students "switching on" their activist thinking.

Assessments

Ms. Lopez views assessments as an important part of the history classroom, but she does not believe that traditional assessments (such as multiple-choice and essay tests) can evaluate students' historical understanding as it relates to justice. She attempts to make her assignments authentic. Her goal is to have students engage in the work of historians (or sociologists, political scientists, or journalists). For instance, in the unit test on abolition of slavery, she asks them to answer the question: "How did slavery last so long in the United States? Using historical evidence, examine the factors that allowed slavery to continue until the end of the Civil War." Unlike a traditional test, where students first see the question on the day of the assessment, Ms. Lopez gives the question to the students at the beginning of the unit. As they learn about abolitionism and the Civil War, they are asked to collect evidence from the class in a folder, which they will be allowed to use on the final assessment. Students are then given 2 days to draft their answer in class, where they also conference with the teacher and their peers. They are allowed to finish the essay outside the classroom, if they need more time. Ms. Lopez says this is a more meaningful way to assess what they know. She states that she knows of no historians who are asked to write an essay about a topic in timed sittings. She wants students to see historical writing as a process, where they plan, receive feedback, and present their best work after substantial thought. She says, "I really want to assess their best work. I don't feel the traditional test does that." She also knows that if they are successful on these more challenging assessments, they will do well on the school's common assessments or the state's history exam.

During her unit on immigration, as a formative assessment, Ms. Lopez has students interview a family or community member who is an immigrant to the United States. The students have to record and transcribe the interview. They then compare their interviewee's immigration story to what they have been learning about the immigrant experience during the early 20th century, as well as the immigration-related current events articles that students had researched. They are asked to make policy recommendations about immigration to the United States today. As a summative assessment, students give presentations on their policy proposals and how their historical study and interview inform their understanding of the issues.

As another example, during her last unit on recent decades, Ms. Lopez asks the students to take a social movement and write its history based on historical evidence. Instead of a traditional research paper, they are allowed to use any type of medium (text, visual arts, music, etc.) to tell the story of a current social movement. Building on the work of Solorzano and Yosso (2002), she describes it as her students' chance to be "counter-storytellers." They are empowered to write the history that they are living in a way that is authentic to their world. One group that chose the killings of unarmed Black and Brown people and the BLM movement decided to write a short hip-hop musical to tell their interpretation of these recent historical events. Another group decided to write their own textbook chapter on Native rights over the past 3 decades from the perspective of Indigenous people.

REFLECTION QUESTIONS

1. What are the strongest justice-oriented aspects of Ms. Lopez's classroom? How might you adapt these techniques for your students?
2. How are the principles of equity and justice apparent inside and outside of Ms. Lopez's history classroom? What other justice-oriented components would you add to her classroom?

3. What are some potential barriers or pitfalls in using social inquiry with high school students? How might teachers overcome those?
4. How does Ms. Lopez integrate the other aspects of social studies (i.e. civics, geography, economics) in her history classroom? How can teachers support justice-oriented social studies instruction?
5. How can field experiences and classroom guests contribute to the preparation of high school students as engaged citizens and activists? Have you designed any of these experiences for your students?

CHAPTER 7

World History at the High School Level

Mr. Tom Kulig

With Maria R. Sequenzia, Framingham Public Schools

The world history classroom can be an important space for teaching justice. Yet it has traditionally served as a tool for oppression. In many nations, the world history curriculum is part of maintaining Eurocentrism and White supremacy (Conrad, 2019; Dozono, in press; Myers, 2006) and patriarchy (Crocco, 2010), especially when it is presented as Western civilization (Dozono, in press; Dunn, 2008). Typically, the whole of world history is framed around European-related events. Students will often only study certain nations or whole continents when a period of time involves European interaction with those places. Moreover, world history textbooks and curriculum portray Europeans as "saviors," providers of global peace and security, and the main drivers of world history (Conrad, 2019; Dozono, in press). They also present non-European people as objects without agency (Dozono, in press). For example, the European invasion and colonization of Africa in the 19th century is often depicted through a White man's burden narrative (Woodward, 1987), which portrays the Europeans as civilizing the African continent (which is, of course, problematic, as numerous African civilizations predate European civilizations, and Africa is a source of much of the knowledge on which European societies were built). Moreover, African resistance to the European invasion is either marginalized in the narrative or completely missing.

As spaces for global citizenship preparation, world history classrooms, especially in the United States, have generally lacked a global perspective (Girard & Harris, 2013; Myers, 2006), and they have often focused on past events that glorify the economic developments and global conquests of European and North American nations (Harris & Girard, 2014). For instance, some of the key events found in most traditional world history courses (and often receiving the most time dedicated to their coverage) include the Columbian exchange, the French Revolution and Napoleon, the industrial revolution (in Europe and the United States, ignoring industrial revolutions elsewhere), European colonization in Africa and Asia, World War I, World War II, and the Cold War; all events that mark periods of European domination and expansion of power.

Traditionally, many world history courses present a "great man" or great individual perspective of the past, where the actions of individual leaders, rather than movements of people, are emphasized. In fact, the debate over whether world history should focus on great individuals or social groups dates back over a century (Ogburn, 1926). We argue in this chapter that for a world history classroom to be justice oriented, it must focus on activists organized in collective movements for change (see Chapter 2). To help students understand how social change happened in the past, they must learn that rarely do "great leaders" or single individuals successfully enact social change by themselves, especially on a global level.

Despite the curricular challenges, there are world history teachers who center global perspectives and teach about the history of their nation-states within a larger global context, as a way to foster global citizenship (Girard & Harris, 2013; Harris & Girard, 2014). These teachers help students learn about world history through a global equity lens, often asking difficult historical questions about power and geography. This chapter attempts to paint a portrait of one of those justice-oriented world history teachers. While the teacher is imagined, he is an amalgamation of practices that we have learned from the numerous world history teachers we have researched over the past decade (Martell, 2013, 2015, 2016, 2017, 2018; Martell & Stevens, 2017a, 2017b; Stevens & Martell, 2016, 2019), or they were practices that we used ourselves as classroom teachers. We hope this illustration offers some important ideas for teachers to consider as they build their classrooms. We start at the beginning of the school year and follow the teacher and their students until the end of the school year.

HISTORY FOR JUSTICE IN THE WORLD HISTORY CLASSROOM

In the United States, world history courses often have a similar rhyme to American history courses in that they center first on the experiences of Europeans and later on the experiences of White Americans. In most world history textbooks, the majority of the chapters relate to European or North American history (often referred to as "the West") and present those histories as separate from the rest of the globe. Common chapter titles include "Classical Greece," "Ancient Rome," "The Formation of Western Europe," "European Renaissance and Reformation," "Nationalist Revolutions Sweep the West," and "Growth of Western Democracies" (Beck et al., 1999; Ellis & Esler, 2005; Ramírez et al., 2008). At the same time, in these textbooks, African, Asian, Middle Eastern, and Indigenous peoples are positioned as global outsiders. Some of the most popular world history textbooks include chapters like, "The Americas: A Separate World," "The Muslim World," "Cultures of East Asia," and "Latin America, Since 1945" (Beck et al., 1999; Ellis & Esler, 2005; Ramírez et al., 2008), as if the people (and their cultures) outside Europe were part of a separate world. In their title and narrative, these chapters do not tend to portray the long histories of interactions and interconnections that most of the world had with Europeans. Instead, the rest of the world is positioned as non-Europeans with their histories often being the result of European actions. Much like textbooks, world history teachers often frame their units around European and North American events and actions, rather than portraying a global story (Girard & Harris, 2013; Harris & Girard, 2014). Moreover, world history teachers are influenced by state standards that typically, and by design, have a Eurocentric orientation (Dozono, in press; Harris, 2014). In fact, attempts to diversify the world curriculum have often been met with political resistance (Nash et al., 2000; Risinger, 1995), especially from those asserting European and White supremacy (Fonte, 1994; Stern, 1994, 1998).

Since much of world history has been influenced by activists and movements for change, it is important that students have an opportunity to analyze the activists' collective work and understand how it led (or did not lead) to our current world. It is important that world history teachers help students see that: (a) people organized in global movements have changed our world, (b) social changes within nation-states were influenced and related to larger global changes, and (c) global events have been influenced by various forms of supremacy (e.g., White supremacy, patriarchy, homophobia/heteronormativity). For instance, the women's suffrage movement in the United States was influenced by the global women's suffrage movement and was only successful due to the collective work of activists, and it faced serious resistance and setbacks as a result of a large mass of people defending the global patriarchy. Moreover, world history teachers should center the voices of people of color (especially Indigenous people and people in the Global South), women, poor and working classes, non-Christian religious groups, and LGBTQ people within their classrooms, and especially when curating sources for students to use in inquiries. Finally, world history teachers should continually ask students to envision a new global community in the present based on fairness (Banks, 2004, 2008). It is not enough to learn about the world's past; teachers should help students connect it to the present and help them imagine a future that aims to solve some of our most pressing problems (e.g., global warming/climate change, poverty, lack of democratic governments).

In this chapter, we intentionally present a vignette of a White teacher working with a predominantly White student population to foster activist thinking and an understanding of movements for change in the past. We see great potential in all history courses to be justice oriented, but it is incredibly important that this work is being done with White students. Systems of oppression have been designed by those groups in power, and they form the tool for maintaining that power; it will need to be people from dominant groups who deconstruct those systems. This is particularly true for White people and racism, but also for men and patriarchy, straight people and heteronormativity, and wealthy people and classism. World history education can help students recognize the roots of oppression and privilege in the past and imagine a society built for everyone in the future.

MR. TOM KULIG'S HIGH SCHOOL WORLD HISTORY CLASSROOM

Mr. Tom Kulig grew up in the suburbs of Chicago, Illinois, where he attended the public schools in a predominantly White and affluent town. His grandparents were immigrants from Poland in the 1920s, and he was raised in a deeply connected Polish American community. From a young age, Tom attended a Catholic church that served as a community center for recent immigrants from Poland. This community, while socially conservative, had a social justice mission for serving the poor and immigrants. After high school, Mr. Kulig majored in history at a large public university in Wisconsin. After graduating, he attended a traditional graduate teacher preparation program at the same university. He was a student teacher at a racially diverse public high school in Madison, Wisconsin, where he taught world history. After completing his master's program, he was hired at a high school in an affluent suburb of Chicago, which was very similar to the community where he grew up. Mr. Kulig is now in his 10th year as a teacher; he teaches world history to 9th- and 10th-grade students. He is the advisor to the school's Gay-Straight Alliance.

Classroom Culture

Before the school year begins, Mr. Kulig is thinking about building a strong culture in his classroom. He wants his classroom to be a space where students can tackle difficult aspects of history and society today in a way that encourages civil debates and perspective taking. While his school has very little racial or class diversity, he focuses his teaching on the school's political diversity. In the last four presidential elections, the town has been divided in its support for the Democratic and Republican candidates. Students have a diverse range of political orientations, including libertarian, conservative, liberal, progressive, and socialist. Despite his students' different political ideologies, he expects all of them to care for others and to think deeply about their own privileges in society. Instead of avoiding politics, he asks students to identify and clarify their political beliefs and use those beliefs to investigate how the world can be made more just.

Being from a similar background and community as his students, Mr. Kulig acknowledges the problems that are caused by the White racial segregation of the school's town, as well as the lack of economic diversity. While the students live near the end of one of Chicago's L (elevated transit system) lines, many rarely visit the city (unless it is to attend attractions, such as sporting events or museums). Many students take vacations outside the country to places in Europe, but rarely Asia, Africa, or Latin America (unless it is to visit a resort). Mr. Kulig knows that this results in his students experiencing a bubble effect, where they think their worldviews and experiences are similar to most people around the world. As such, he designs his course around global history and authentic experiences from African, Asian, Middle Eastern, and Indigenous peoples. At the same time, he works carefully to not essentialize the experiences of those groups that his students have limited knowledge of and have had few interactions with. He carefully builds lessons that show the diversity of different groups' views and experiences throughout history.

Pedagogical Approaches

While Mr. Kulig uses many different techniques in his classroom, his pedagogy is most aligned with what Martell (2018) described as *discovering*, "where a teacher views the role as presenting different cultural perspectives of the past or present and then allows the students to make interpretations" (p. 69). His main goal is to help students "understand their own identities and cultures, while also encouraging students to view the content of social studies as composed of many competing, diverse perspectives" (Martell & Stevens, 2019, p. 6). Importantly, he designs his lessons with an emphasis on the experiences of nondominant groups and how privilege frames the experiences of members of dominant groups (which most of his students belong to); he does not believe that content is neutral (Bagget & Simmons, 2017). He often asks his students to use a political lens when examining the past. He values inquiry-based instruction and has his students routinely answer historical questions using evidence. However, he is not the only person in his classroom asking the questions. Much like the teacher in the previous chapter, early in the school year, Mr. Kulig has his students practice asking their own historical questions, and he encourages them to become acquainted with different source repositories, so they can eventually take the lead on the historical inquiries. His inquiry is a process to analyze historical events using different social lenses with the intention of developing empathy and challenging preconceived notions of the past. He explains to his students that learning should involve investigations of the past, where they should act as their own historians, scrutinizing evidence and using their ideologies to make interpretations of the past (while also considering how people of different political ideologies or social identities may have viewed events differently in the past and today).

During the school year, Mr. Kulig focuses on how various forms of supremacy have influenced events in the past. In the beginning of the year, he focuses on White, male, wealthy, and straight privilege. He asks students to examine the social identities of people and structures of societies over time. In this, he knows it is very important for them to see that social identities and structures have never been static, and they are often being defined and redefined by societies. Mr. Kulig has students continually assess the prevailing views of race, class, gender, sexual orientation, and religion within various societies over certain periods. For example, he routinely asks them to think about a particular society's view of sexual orientation (e.g., same-sex relationships in ancient Greece, some ancient Chinese leaders being openly gay or bisexual, Nandi women in East Africa since the 18th century having the ability to marry other women, the concept of Two-Spirit among the Diné [Navajo] people that existed before European colonization). He then has them trace when being gay, lesbian, bisexual, or transgender was permitted or not permitted in societies (and who had freedom in sexual orientation and who did not).

Curriculum

Mr. Kulig finds strategic ways to use the skills listed in the state-mandated history curriculum to teach history for justice. The state social studies standards in Illinois do not include specific social studies content for most grade levels. Each district and school can determine the content necessary for each course, with the state requiring two social studies courses at the high school level with at least one year of U.S. history and government. In some ways, the standards are liberating, as they allow Mr. Kulig and his department flexibility in what courses are offered. However, they have also noticed that social studies is often considered less important than other subjects, such as English, which is required every year.

Unit 1: The Beginning of Humankind. During the first week of school, Mr. Kulig has the students examine biological and anthropological research on the origins of humans to write the history of the common ancestors (sometimes colloquially referred to as Y-chromosomal Adam and mitochondrial Eve). Students learn that humans' common ancestors were from Africa (likely the Great Rift Valley) and possibly lived during similar times but were not mates. They had the ability to make tools and fire, and they could also communicate. In the following lesson, Mr. Kulig has the students look at human migration and how people spread throughout the world. Students also debate the possible routes that Native peoples in the Americas took during their migration from Asia.

Unit 2: Ancient Global Societies. Unlike traditional world history courses that organize their units around particular regions, Mr. Kulig's course is organized around global connections during various eras of time. For instance, he does not have a separate unit on ancient Greece, but instead he has students examine numerous communities around the world between the 6th and 10th centuries BCE, including the Egyptians, Babylonians, Chinese, Mayans, Nok, and Greeks. To accomplish this, he often has students engage in various types of historical research projects on different groups from an era and then compare the development of those societies over time. In their research, students are asked to look at different social groups, searching for issues of inequity or injustice, and then examine how groups of people mobilized for social change.

Unit 3: The Medieval Period. In the next unit, Mr. Kulig has the students study the medieval period. However, unlike how it is presented in most textbooks or curricula as a primarily European era, he has them examine this era as a period of globalization; they learn about how Europe was connected to the rest of the world by a global network, which also reveals how some African, Asian, and Indigenous societies were far more advanced at this time. For example, students perform "historical dives" into various global events, including Sei Shōnagon and other women in the Japanese court organizing for gender equity or the establishment of the great libraries of Timbuktu. Students also learn about the global spread of the bubonic plague, including how it impacted social inequity in various places (including peasant uprisings), and they consider if it was a possible impetus for later European colonization. They also investigate the European and American witch hunts, which involved widespread gendercide and gender inequity during the period.

The unit ends with a series of lessons on the history of Islam, where Mr. Kulig has students engage in a textbook rewrite project. He wants them to see the embedded dominant narratives found in the educational materials that they use in school. Instead of assigning textbooks to his students, he asks them to locate the chapter on "The Rise of Islam" and, in groups, to rewrite it from a Muslim and Middle Eastern perspective, using primary sources and art from the Middle East or created by Muslims. The narrative is centered on the Muslim and Middle Eastern perspective, and European and other perspectives can be put in a sidebar (similar to how nondominant perspectives are placed in the sidebars of many U.S. textbooks). As part of that project, students must also grapple with the European Crusades from the Islamic perspective. They examine one of Europe's early attempts at worldwide conquest and colonization (as Dunbar-Ortiz [2015] called it, a dress rehearsal for the later colonization of the Americas), and how the people of the Middle East resisted and sustained their religion and culture during that period. They viewed clips from the Al Jazeera English (2016) special *The Crusades: An Arab Perspective.*

The students become incredibly engaged in the activity. They search for videos of Middle Eastern historians on the Internet for better context.

Mr. Kulig gives them excerpts from Tamim Ansary's (2009) *Destiny Disrupted: A History of the World Through Islamic Eyes*. They use the "Internet Islamic History Sourcebook" from Fordham University as a main place to find sources to include in their revised textbook chapters. Before the final chapters are written, the students must critique each other's work, and a scholar of Islamic history at a local university visits the class, giving final feedback on the chapters and serving as a resource for the students as they complete their texts. In the end, the chapters will be printed and deposited in the school library, so other students can read the students' work.

Unit 4: The Era of Revolutions. When Mr. Kulig starts planning his next unit on 18th- and 19th-century revolutions, he decides to incorporate that same type of analysis, while also stressing the links between events that happen years apart. From his own education, Mr. Kulig remembers clearly the focus on the French Revolution. Highlighted as a paradigm of people responding to an unjust government and the successor to the American Revolution, it is actually the only other revolution Mr. Kulig remembers studying as a high school student. To remedy that for his students, Mr. Kulig tries a new approach. Instead of having them learn about revolutions in an isolated manner, as if they each happened in a vacuum, he designs a project where students—as they typically do—will begin by learning about the French Revolution. But then, instead of continuing on with European wars and unifications, he plans to have his students research subsequent revolutions on other continents, some relating to European aggression or colonization, and others not. Some of the revolutions, such as the Haitian Revolution (1791) and the Cần Vương movement (1885), involved movements of oppressed peoples against the French (the same nation that declared "liberty, equality, fraternity!" for its own people) or against other European powers, like the Yihetuan Movement/Boxer Rebellion (1899–1901) or the Philippine Revolution (1896–1898). Other movements were about preserving culture, language, and religion, or they were an attempt to change the social order, such as the Fula jihads in Nigeria and Cameroon (1804–1808), the Korean peasant rebellion (1811), the Rebellions in French Canada (1837–1838), the Caste War of Yucatán (1847–1901), and the Xinhai Revolution in China (1911).

Through this unit, Mr. Kulig hopes his students will take away the nuance that it is important to detect when learning history. It is easier for students to initially sympathize with the French Third Estate, which was protesting regressive taxes and an unfair social hierarchy. However, over the next hundred years, iterations of that very group of people and their government (and others in Europe) that triumphed over tyranny will become the tyrants, expanding slavery and crushing any civil disobedience. Meanwhile, Indigenous, African, and Asian people will lead revolutions of their own, which are unrelated to European aggression. Mr. Kulig hopes to present a more complex view of this era of revolutions, so that students can critically analyze how oppression sustains itself and perpetuates inequity over time, and also how people resist by protecting and sustaining their cultures.

Mr. Kulig also believes it is crucial for his students to understand that when some groups in societies gain rights or power, other groups may be losing their rights or power; history is not always a march forward into progress. To illustrate this, he has students participate in a role-playing activity of the Estates General during the period of the French Revolution, which is a common activity in many world history courses. However, he adds a twist; halfway through the simulation, he has several students join as representatives of the groups who were persecuted by the French government over the following century and did not have any say in French governance during this era of expanded democracy. From the Caribbean, there are representatives from the Haitian Revolution (and their leaders Toussaint Louverture and Jean-Jacques Dessalines) and enslaved people from Martinique who led an uprising in 1831. From Asia, Tôn Thất Thuyết of the Cần Vương movement in Vietnam shares an early perspective on their attempt to expel the French, and Wu Tingfang represents a Chinese perspective on European influence in his country. The project allows students to analyze the connections between France's revolution and the subsequent revolutions against France, but it also gives students a chance to perspective-take through activists and associated freedom movements.

Unit 5: Global Conflicts. In the next unit, Mr. Kulig has the students investigate the world at war in the first half of the 20th century. Instead of having them focus on battles or the decisions of world leaders, which is the traditional approach, he has students focus on the impacts on everyday people during two global conflicts bookending a worldwide depression. Each student takes on the persona of a real person who lived through the period, and they must journal about their experiences and views on world events. Mr. Kulig intentionally chooses people from all continents (except Antarctica), women and men, young and old, straight and queer (including a trans person living in Germany). The students examine such complex issues as colonized people being forced to fight for imperial armies, people surviving hunger and pandemics, resistance movements to fascism and authoritarianism, and genocide. He intentionally avoids a Hollywood-like portrayal of the world wars as heroic, and instead he shows students how the wars led to extensive violence and inequity.

Unit 6: Supremacy and Liberation. In the last unit, Mr. Kulig frames the mid-20th century as a tension between supremacists and liberation movements. This begins with a mini-unit on African sovereignty. Unlike the traditional world history courses, which have a unit on European imperialism that starts and ends with the European division of the continent (and can be the last time that many students learn about Africa), this unit covers from European colonization in the 1800s to national independence in the 1900s, and it explains a more complete timeline ending with African empowerment. The unit then shifts to a culminating project where students analyze the fundamental parts of various 20th-century social movements around the globe.

They start with social movements that they have studied previously (e.g., women's rights in the 10th-century Japanese court, peasant uprisings during the bubonic plague, Haitian Revolution, Fula jihads, Yihetuan Movement), which they will use as models to analyze a social movement from the 20th century. The students answer the following questions regarding the movements that they studied throughout the year:

- Did a group of people at the time want to change society, and did they have a vision for how it might look different? If so, what was that vision and how was it different?
- Did a group of people at the time outline and help educate the public about a particular type of oppression and the ways that they could work against it? Did they make the case to the public that alternatives to the status quo would benefit all?
- Did a group of people at the time engage in collective actions? (Was there a "trigger event" that gained public attention? What methods were used to raise public awareness?) Did the movement gain public support? Did the group's collective actions lead to a change in society? Is there still a legacy of this today?

After that, the students work in small groups to research their assigned activist groups, which represent various groups from around the world in the 20th century, such as apartheid in South Africa, Indigenous rights movements in Brazil and Australia, freedom movements in Asia and Eastern Europe, and various civil rights movements (civil rights for African Americans, women's liberation, LGBTQ rights, immigrant rights) in the United States and Canada. The students then work together to outline the phases of their assigned social movements and create an overview of the path that a movement takes. They create presentations in a variety of formats to explain how their movement both followed and deviated from typical movements' paths. This project helps students create models for different types of activism, which hopefully will enable them to envision social change in their own world and prepare and participate in possible collective action.

After developing a strong foundation of world history, the students organize and host, with Mr. Kulig's help, a global justice fair for the school community where they educate schoolmates and the public on various current global issues that are rooted in past historical events. The purpose of the event is to imagine a better world 50 years from now and the steps that would need to be taken by movements. For example, one student group presents on the unfair labor practices of sneaker companies today and the historical connection to European colonialism and rubber production. They built their project around Hochschild's (1999) *King Leopold's Ghost: A Story of Greed, Terror and Heroism in Colonial Africa*. Another group discusses the impact that climate change is having on Pacific Islanders. They feature images collected by the National Geographic Foundation that show the environmental impact in places such as Kiribati, Vanuatu, Tuvalu, Marshall Islands, and Solomon Islands. Mr. Kulig encourages the students to extend their work beyond the classroom and get involved with local grassroots organizations doing work related to these social issues.

Unit 7: Recent Global History. Mr. Kulig had planned to end the year with a unit on recent history from a global perspective, which would have included the collapse of the Soviet Union, genocide in Rwanda, global terrorism, climate change, and the development of global pop culture (such as the rise of Japanese anime, K-pop, Bollywood, and the global popularity of African European hip-hop and Caribbean reggaeton). However, like so many other schools around the world in 2020, Mr. Kulig's school closes in March due to the COVID-19 pandemic. Eager to continue remote instruction, but also very aware of the toll this is taking on his students' mental and emotional health, Mr. Kulig designs a project for students to process what is happening around them, while creating a historical record in which they are participants, rather than simply observers. The project allows the students to use a variety of methods to analyze the social, economic, and political impacts of COVID-19. In his first remote class, Mr. Kulig explains that they are creating a historical record for future historians; the students are to create journals and poems about how their lives are changing, and they should interview family members to create oral histories. A group of students creates a news program–style video interviewing historians and epidemiologists about past pandemics. Another group analyzes the differences in the economic impacts in countries on each continent and creates a blog comparing different governments' responses (including their own government's response). Two other groups examine the widespread racism that was embedded in the response, with one covering the anti–Asian American racism and violence, and another analyzing the discrepancies in health outcomes for Black and Latinx people. While the COVID-19 pandemic presents a very difficult way to end the year, Mr. Kulig uses it as a moment to help his students examine injustice and inequity in their current time.

Field Experiences and Classroom Guests

Mr. Kulig knows how important it is, especially in a world history course, to have his students "leave the bubble" of their predominantly White suburban community. He routinely takes them on field experiences outside their community and has people from other communities visit his classroom. In this, he is very careful in trying to avoid othering, especially when it comes to learning about people of color. To do this, he works to bring guests to his classroom and bring his students to places outside their community.

For example, midway through the year during the unit on industrialism and imperialism at the turn of the 20th century, Mr. Kulig uses the 1893 World's Columbian Exposition in Chicago to teach about global injustice. He starts the unit by taking his students on a field trip to the Chicago History Museum, where they examine artifacts and sources related to the exposition, which was a fair to celebrate Columbus's so-called discovery of the Americas. There students learn about the Exhibition's nickname, the "White City" (with its double meaning: white buildings and White perspectives), with its exclusion of African Americans from the Exhibition's leadership (Paddon & Turner, 1995; Rudwick & Meier, 1965). Mr. Kulig has students examine the problematic (and racist) depictions of African, Asian, Middle Eastern, and Indigenous people at the fair in the various displays of humans in a zoo-like fashion (Sutter, 2018) and the racist tropes found in *Harper's Weekly* coverage of an African American family visiting the fair (Cooks, 2007), which were used to maintain established racial hierarchies. The students are surprised and disturbed by the overt racism. Some even begin to make connections to the portrayal of Black people in current-day media. However, concerned that his predominantly White students might think of Africans and African Americans as victims of the past, he moves the discussion to Black resistance and protest. The students learn about the Haitian Pavilion, which was used by Frederick Douglass, Ida B. Wells, Ferdinand Lee Barnet, Irvine Garland Penn, and others (Reed, 2002) to mobilize against the racism of the Exhibition. They read a pamphlet that the Black activists created, titled *The Reason Why the Colored American Is Not in the World's Columbian Exposition*. In having them do so, Mr. Kulig carefully exposes the students to these materials, being very mindful of the racism embedded within them. He intentionally uses this as a moment to show his predominantly White students how White people in the past used racist media as a tool to oppress people of color. At the same time, he is especially mindful that the small population of students of color (but also White students) may be negatively affected by seeing these racist images, so he allows any students to opt out of viewing these materials.

Each quarter, Mr. Kulig has a guest or panel come and speak to his students about life today in the places whose history they are studying. This includes a community member who grew up in Palestine (during the unit on the spread of Islam) and a panel of Jewish Holocaust survivors (during the unit on the world wars). When the students are studying the independence movements in Africa (as part of a larger unit on global civil rights), he invites a local Ghanaian American photographer who documents Chicago's

West African community with her camera. Mr. Kulig wants his students to better understand how strong the West African diaspora is in Chicago and how the various West African communities in the area today relate to the independence movements that they have been studying. Before the students arrive, the photographer posts her photographs (most of whose subjects are first- or second-generation immigrants from West Africa) around the room. When Mr. Kulig's students enter the room, he asks them to engage in a gallery walk, where they should write at least one question they have about each photograph. These questions are then used to interview the photographer, asking her not only about the photographs but also, more importantly, about the stories of the people she captured. The photographer discusses the differences, but also the shared connections, among the Senegalese, Nigerian, Malian, and Ghanaian Americans in Chicago. For many of the students, this was a powerful activity; learning the stories of migration from local people through images evoked important senses of empathy.

Despite the thought that he put into his world history classroom, Mr. Kulig's school year was not without some controversies. In November, about a week after the Islam textbook chapter rewrite project was finished, Mr. Kulig gets a voice mail from a parent. The message says, "Mr. Kulig, this is Jim Russo, Tyler's father. I would like to talk to you about a recent project in your class that has me very concerned. Please call me back as soon as possible." Mr. Kulig returns the call, which leads to a 20-minute discussion. The parent tells Mr. Kulig that he is very troubled by the fact that Tyler is learning about Islam in his class. Mr. Kulig tells Mr. Russo that teaching about Islam is part of the school's world history curriculum. Mr. Russo says, "Yeah, I get that, but the way you are teaching it, I think you are teaching our kids to become Muslims." Mr. Kulig is a bit confused and probes further. The parent tells him that by having students take the perspectives of Muslims, they are teaching them that Islam is right and their religion is wrong. Sensing that this conversation is not heading in a productive direction, Mr. Kulig tells the parent that he must get back to teaching, and he suggests that this may need to be a larger conversation with his department head or others in the school. The parent agrees.

A week later, Mr. Kulig meets with the parent, the department head, and the school's principal. They listen to the parent, who is much calmer. Mr. Kulig explains that students learn about most major world religions, including Islam, which is the world's second-largest religion of almost 2 billion people. He explains that rarely are historians of Islam involved in writing textbooks, and this assignment is to help students see perspectives that are often missing. Mr. Kulig knows that there have been several media outlets and organizations encouraging parents to demand that Islam not be taught or that it be taught as a religion of violent extremists in their children's schools (Green, 2015), which troubles him. He is very careful to explain that his class is not teaching theology, but instead comparative religion. At the end of the meeting, Mr. Russo says that he is still concerned, but that he at least has a better understanding of what is happening in the classroom.

Assessments

Mr. Kulig knows that there are many ways that students can demonstrate their knowledge and understanding of the past. He is committed to providing opportunities for authentic assessments that allow students to show what they have learned by applying it to the real world. By engaging in this type of thinking (labeled cultural preparation in Chapter 2), they imagine what society could be like—envisioning a new society in which traditional oppressive structures do not exist. He also knows that it is important to engage students' connection to popular culture, and specifically popular culture that presents perspectives different than their own. Therefore, Mr. Kulig has an in-class showing of the film *Black Panther* (Coogler, 2018), and then students analyze the film from a historical and social standpoint; they analyze the story line, historical analogies, social significance, and potential activist and movement-related aspects. To do this, they must interpret historical documents about colonization and African independence movements. They must imagine an alternate future for Africa, like Wakanda in the film, that is based on African intellectual history and is free of European imperialism. They connect this project back to the field trip that they took to the Chicago History Museum, where they looked at some of the historical roots of anti-African thinking. The students are encouraged to use a multimodal approach to their presentation, and they have a level of creative freedom for the finished product. Some students make models, create a journal including a critical essay, or write and perform songs. One group presents spoken word involving interspliced dialogue from the movie interspersed with lines from enslaved people in the Belgian Congo and the African National Congress. Another group creates a series of posters illustrating the specific ways in which the absence of European imperialism would have led to a very different reality for Africa and the world.

REFLECTION QUESTIONS

1. What are the strongest justice-oriented aspects of Mr. Kulig's classroom? How might you adapt these techniques for your students?
2. How are the principles of equity and justice apparent inside and outside of Mr. Kulig's history classroom? What other justice-oriented components would you add to his classroom?
3. What are some potential barriers or pitfalls in using social inquiry with high school students? How might teachers overcome those?

4. How does Mr. Kulig integrate the other aspects of social studies (i.e., civics, geography, economics) in his history classroom? How can teachers support justice-oriented social studies instruction?

5. How can field experiences and classroom guests contribute to the preparation of high school students as engaged citizens and activists? Have you designed any of these experiences for your students?

CHAPTER 8

Ancient World History at the Middle Level

Ms. Joyce Smith

With Neema Avashia, Boston Public Schools

The ancient history classroom can be an important space for teaching justice. However, as it has been traditionally taught, ancient history rarely focuses on justice, and it generally lacks a connection to the current lives of students. Most ancient history courses in North America and Europe focus heavily on ancient Greece and Rome. They also place non-European societies within the sphere of Europe (such as the Mesopotamians or Egyptians, who are depicted culturally as European-like or with lighter skin colors to appear White). This has taught generations of students that the world was built, from the so-called beginnings of civilization, by and for wealthy European straight men. They make up the heroes; they are credited with the greatest political, philosophical, and artistic achievements.

White supremacy was intentionally built into the original design of ancient history courses. These courses became standard components of North American and European education in the 18th and 19th centuries (Marino, 2010; Morris & Scheidel, 2016), at a time when those nations were first engaging in colonialism and later in imperialism. Eurocentric ancient history was used to justify the emerging national boundaries and related nationalism (Hourdakis, 1996; Hourdakis et al., 2018), especially in Western Europe, the United States, and Canada; it was to show that these nations were the heirs to civilization started in Greece and Rome. Moreover, Eurocentric ancient history was used to justify White people's global power and expansion, as well as assert European and American exceptionalism. For instance, the study of Greek and Roman history, as proof of European superiority, was advocated by Herbert Spencer, who was a lead developer of scientific racism in the late 1800s (Morris & Scheidel, 2016). In the 1980s and 1990s, Eurocentric ancient history again gained popularity and was advocated for by a group of scholars and politicians, often politically conservative, as a way to combat the emergence of multicultural education in the 1960s and 1970s (Dunn, 2008; Nash et al., 2000). They argued that for national unity, it was essential that all Americans learn that the U.S. government, and more broadly civilization, was originally founded in Europe and built on a Western heritage and culture (Gagnon, 1998; Ravitch, 1990; Ravitch & Finn, 1987; Stotsky, 2004). Yet that is an inaccurate understanding of the ancient world. Human civilizations developed on all continents (except Antarctica) simultaneously, and some of the ancient civilizations in Africa, Asia, and the Americas were more sophisticated than their European contemporaries (Dunbar-Ortiz, 2015; Irani & Silver, 1995). Moreover, it also ignores evidence that the United States borrowed ideas from outside Europe (Dunbar-Ortiz, 2015; Irani & Silver, 1995). Finally, it ignores that humankind has had one shared history from the beginning of our existence (Hourdakis, 1996). It intentionally distorts human commonality to justify human segregation and a hierarchy that places Whites, and their histories and cultures, at the top.

Instead, we argue that there is no better place to teach history for justice than the ancient history classroom. In fact, Indigenous, African, Asian, and European conceptions of justice were established during this ancient era of human history (Dunbar-Ortiz, 2015; Irani & Silver, 1995). There are numerous examples found across the continents of people organized in movements for social change. However, students often find ancient history irrelevant to their lives because of the curriculum's traditional format (Endacott, 2005). Yet there are teachers who help students see ancient world history as global and multicultural (Choi, 2013). They center ancient history on the origin of humankind, human migration, the development of civilizations, and the beginnings of globalization (Choi, 2013; Endacott, 2005). By doing so, they also better help students see how that ancient world led to our present one (Choi, 2013; Endacott, 2005).

It is particularly important for middle school students to have opportunities to critically examine and understand the ancient world in relation to their own social identities and the social identities of others. In early adolescence, students are in a pivotal point in their racial, gender, and sexual identities (Jones et al., 2019; Manning, 1993; Tatum, 1997). There is evidence that positive racial identity development, especially for students of color, has an impact on their academic and social success (DuBois et al., 2002; Helms, 1990, 1995; Holcomb-McCoy, 2005; Manning, 1993). Helms (1990, 1995) argued that a positive identity for people of color leads to a recognition of internalized societal racial stereotypes, offering a path to overcome them while also gaining solidarity with other oppressed peoples. She contended that a positive identity for White people means that they acknowledge their Whiteness and how it frames their lived experience, including their social privilege, and make a commitment to actively work against racial oppression. Similarly, this is the period in people's lives when they are developing positive social identities related to their sexual orientation and gender identities (Jones et al., 2019; Manning, 1993). It is a time when students are making sense of the current world and who they are within it. As such, this must be when students develop an appreciation for the long histories of their people and how other groups' histories interacted with, and in some cases disrupted, their ancestors. Ultimately, this will allow them to draw a bright line between the ancient past and their present experiences. It will help them develop pride in who they are as descendants of their ancestors. It will reveal stories and examples, especially for students from groups experiencing oppression, of how collectively their ancestors sustained their communities.

HISTORY FOR JUSTICE IN THE ANCIENT HISTORY CLASSROOM

Ancient histories may be the most difficult topics to teach in the history classroom. Since these periods occurred long ago and in a world that was very different from our own, students often find understanding these periods to be difficult. Yet for some students, a topic's strangeness might make it particularly interesting. Like modern history, ancient history has been strongly influenced by movements. People in the ancient past often worked together to end oppression and seek freedom. If teachers approached ancient world history with an emphasis on fairness and equity, then we contend that many more students would find it not only relevant to their lives, but also more interesting. Learning about the collective struggle of the people, rather than the triumphs of powerful individuals, is a much more compelling story. Since many people will claim certain components of our world were formed in ancient times, it is essential for students to learn the complexities of how our current world was shaped by people who lived thousands of years ago; this includes dark moments in history, but also moments of social progress led by ancient activists (while the word *activist* only dates back to the early 20th century, direct action by the people has existed through most of human history).

In this chapter, we present a vignette that illustrates what teaching history for justice can look like in a middle school ancient history classroom. We attempt to show how the study of peoples from over a millennium ago can help students understand activism and social movements today. While the teacher is imagined, she is an amalgamation of practices that we have learned from the numerous middle school history teachers we have researched over the past decade (Martell, 2013, 2015, 2016, 2017, 2018; Martell & Stevens, 2017a, 2017b; Stevens & Martell, 2016, 2019), or they were practices that we used ourselves as classroom teachers. We hope this illustration offers some important ideas for teachers to consider as they build their classrooms.

MS. JOYCE SMITH'S MIDDLE SCHOOL ANCIENT
HISTORY CLASSROOM

Ms. Joyce Smith grew up in Charleston, West Virginia, where she attended the public schools. Her grandparents came to West Virginia from Alabama and Georgia during the Great Migration in the 1920s. Ms. Smith was raised in a close-knit and relatively small Black community. From a young age, she attended services at the local Baptist church, which was the spiritual and social anchor of her community. Many of the community's elders were engaged in activism during and after the civil rights era.

After high school, she majored in history at a large private university in New York. It was a major culture shock. Coming from a relatively small city in a rural part of the country and going to one of the world's megalopolises was eye-opening. At the same time, it was liberating. As an African American growing up in a predominantly White area, she had few experiences with people who looked like her outside her church community. In New York, she experienced the diversity of New York's Black communities. For the first time, she met Black people who came from the Caribbean, West Africa, and East Africa. It helped her gain a more complex understanding of her Blackness and her own family's histories.

She decided to remain in New York City for an additional year and received her teaching license and a master's degree through a yearlong urban residency teacher preparation program, which was a district-university partnership. As a student teacher, she worked at a middle school in the Bronx where she taught U.S. and New York history. In the following fall, she found a full-time position as a 7th-grade social studies teacher at a middle school in Brooklyn. She loved teaching students who came from all over the world. Her teacher preparation program had focused on culturally relevant pedagogy, which she built her own classroom around. She learned to listen to her students, and she learned from the students' stories of themselves, their families, and their ancestors. After 5 years of working in the New York City public schools, Ms. Smith began to miss her family and home. She decided to return to Charleston, and she took a job in one of the city's middle schools. While the school was predominantly White, a quarter of the students were Black, and there was a small population of Latinx and Asian students.

Ms. Smith is now in her seventh year as a teacher; she teaches ancient history and world geography to 7th-grade students. She is the advisor to the school's Black Student Union. In many ways, her students in West Virginia were very different from her students in New York. In West Virginia, most of her students were born and raised in Charleston. They infrequently traveled to larger cities, such as Pittsburgh, Cincinnati, and Charlotte, as they were over 3 hours away. She was, in some ways, returning to a bubble; granted, it was a familiar bubble. Having grown up in Charleston, she knew many of the students' families, and she understood their experiences growing up. She knew that her students were much more likely to have experience in the outdoors compared to her former students in New York, and she tried to connect ancient history to the natural world because of it. In many ways, being from the community helped her approach difficult and controversial topics with her students. They trusted her as a community insider. At the same time, her experiences in New York helped her see the importance of opening up a global understanding for her students.

Classroom Culture

At the end of the previous school year, Ms. Smith sets up conferences with her incoming students. She visits them in their 6th-grade social studies classroom and has a short conversation, which helps her get to know them. Although many of the students have older siblings who have been in Ms. Smith's class, and others know her from church and the community, Ms. Smith knows the importance of *building* a classroom community, rather than simply relying on existing relationships. This is one way that she can learn about who her new students are and about their interests. Ms. Smith also knows that this is very important for gaining the students' trust. In her classroom, they will grapple with difficult histories, and she works hard to establish a rapport with all of her students early on, so they can take intellectual risks. She believes in her students, which results in her continuously challenging them in a caring way. One student called her "a real brain stretcher," but one who loved them all.

At the start of the school year, Ms. Smith invests in relationship and community building during her early lessons, knowing that this early investment will lead to deeper learning, and less disruption, later. For example, Ms. Smith starts one early lesson by sharing her "identity tree" with students—pictures and stories about her own identity—and then she asks them to create and share their own identity trees. She makes it clear that her classroom is a place where students can be their full selves, and where she will be transparent about her own identity as well.

Ms. Smith also strives to teach her students to make the familiar strange and the strange familiar. She deems this an essential part of teaching ancient civilization. Her hope is that by the end of the year her students will have moved away from ethnocentric thinking and will examine cultures through a cultural relativist's lens. One way she does this is by starting the year having her students read an article on the Nacirema people. In the article, an anthropologist studies this culture and describes the group's many rituals and practices, which may seem strange to the students. Members of the Nacirema community use hairs in their mouth in a formalized series of gestures that have magical powers. Ms. Smith asks the students to comment on this tribe and their rituals. Many of them react with comments about how these rituals are weird or gross. After the discussion, Ms. Smith explains that Nacirema is actually America spelled backward, and the behaviors and practices described are those the students do every day, such as brushing their teeth. The discussion and the article make a clear point that we often view cultures through an ethnocentric lens rather than from a place of understanding. Ms. Smith often refers to the Nacirema article throughout the year when she hears judgmental comments from her students when they study ancient civilizations.

Pedagogical Approaches

While Ms. Smith uses many different pedagogical techniques in her classroom, her pedagogy is most aligned with what Martell (2018) described as *exchanging,*

> where a teacher views his or her role as facilitating discussions that help students make sense of race and culture. The teacher will encourage students to use their own lived experiences to better understand the content, which may include counter-storytelling (Chandler, 2015; Solorzano & Yosso, 2002) that often raises questions about the dominant portrayals of the past and present. (p. 67)

She aims to develop within her students "a more inclusive collective memory," and she also aims to develop an "increased cultural understanding among all students through critical conversations" (Martell & Stevens, 2019, p. 6). This means that she must help her White students grapple with how their ancestors' choices and actions, starting in the ancient world, led to an accumulation of social power and privileges in today's world.

Simultaneously, Ms. Smith engages in what Duncan (2019) called emancipatory pedagogies for her Black students. As one of the few Black teachers in the school, she wants to ensure that Black students have a teacher with high expectations for them, see the positive historical contributions of Black people, and develop a critical lens on the world. She wants all of her students to learn that one way to correct those past injustices is by advocating for fairness and equity in the present. She also helps her students of color as they examine the stories of their ancestors and how many of their current traditions and cultural views may have begun a long time ago. At the same time, she wants her students of color to see how systems of power were constructed, which can help explain the current injustices in society and the ways that they may be changed.

Ms. Smith also knows the importance of having regular inter- and intra-racial dialogues in the classroom (Busey, 2014; Howard & del Rosario, 2000; King & Chandler, 2016), providing students ample opportunities to talk within their groups, but also with students from different racial backgrounds. At the same time, she knows it is crucial to never put students on the spot or ask them to be the representative of their various social identities. Instead, she reminds her students that they only can speak for themselves and their experiences. Ms. Smith is mindful of race and gender when creating partnerships and groups in her classroom. She balances between opportunities when students get to choose and when she chooses for them, which ensures the young people in her classroom have intentional opportunities to interact across backgrounds.

Curriculum

Ms. Smith finds strategic ways to use the skills listed in the state-mandated middle school history curriculum to teach history for justice. The state social studies standards in West Virginia do not include specific social studies content at most grade levels, and 7th grade is generally a study of ancient and modern civilizations. Each district and school can determine the content necessary for each course, so Ms. Smith works with her fellow social studies teachers to create a course focusing on the ancient world across the Americas, Africa, Asia, and Europe. It is essentially what Endacott (2005) called society studies, where students compare different civilizations over time, based on similar factors, such as health care and practices, trade, religion, government, or social structures. When they create their school's curriculum map, Ms. Smith and her colleagues present a series of through-line questions that they might adopt, where each unit of the course during the year would look at these same questions about the civilization being studied:

- How did this society define justice?
- How did their social structures change (and over time did society improve or become worse for the people)?
- What was this society's view of religion, and how did it change over time?
- What was this society's view of government, and how did it change over time?
- How did this society develop technology over time?
- What role did art and culture play in this society?

The teachers also decide that every unit must connect ancient peoples to their current-day diasporas. In this endeavor, Ms. Smith works hard to center authentic voices, especially those of the Indigenous peoples, people of color, women, the poor and working classes, and LGBTQ people. This can be particularly difficult in ancient world history, as the historical record is often incomplete because it was damaged, lost, or never recorded (unintentionally or intentionally). As such, Ms. Smith often relies on images and artwork to elevate the voices of the people from ancient times, as well as relying on powerful secondary sources created by anthropologists and historians. When sources are not available, she will often ask students to imagine what a person during this period might have thought or done based on the evidence they have available. She engages students in their historical imaginations, realizing that history is based on evidence, but that evidence is often far from complete.

Ms. Smith also takes a case-study approach to ancient history, where she intentionally begins with Africa (as it is where humans began), which is followed by Asia and the Americas. She does this to acknowledge that humankind began in Africa and because Africa is rarely included in the PreK-12 curriculum (Dillard et al., 2017). Traditionally, ancient world history dedicates most of the course to the European content; it often focuses primarily on (or sometimes begins with) the ancient Greeks and Romans. This intentionally presents Europeans as the creators of civilization and then allows for the justification of their later colonization and conquering of other people in the name of spreading civilization. Ms. Smith does not want to frame ancient history through European violence. Instead, she reimagines history as an arc of sustaining cultures. She wants students to know that human history is a history of resistance and struggle, but also creation and advancement, and no one continent had the monopoly on civilization. She wants her White students to learn that the racist system that privileges Whites and demonizes foreigners was conceived in the ancient world (Delacampagne, 1983; Isaac, 2004), has changed over time, and, despite its longevity, can be undone today. At the same time, she wants her students of color to receive messages from the curriculum that they do not come from a defeated group. Rather, their ancestors come from deep and long-lasting intellectual and cultural traditions created in the ancient world. While Europeans may have tried to erase and replace their histories, their cultures persist, and, by learning about the histories of their ancestors, they are inheriting something important from their ancestors.

Unit 1: Human Origins. During the first unit of the school year, Ms. Smith has students examine the beginnings of humankind. She breaks it down into three mini-units: one on the beginning of the Earth, one on the beginning of humans, and one on the beginning of distinct cultures. For the first homework assignment, Ms. Smith starts by having students ask their families the following question: "How did the world begin? How did humankind begin?" They then spend the next day compiling and comparing their families' human and world origin stories. The next day, Ms. Smith has students examine the prevailing scientific theories on how the universe and world began, including research on the formation of the Earth and the supercontinent of Pangaea. The students compare the scientific and cultural ideas, answering the larger philosophical question, "Why do people wonder about the origins of the world?" Ms. Smith intentionally begins this course by focusing on the prehuman Earth, as she wants the students to gain an understanding that humans have existed for only a very small period of time. She has the students watch a video showing the world's history as a 24-hour day with humans appearing in the last second.

Next, Ms. Smith turns to the mini-unit on the beginning of humankind. She starts by presenting the biological and anthropological research on the origins of humans to write the history of the common ancestors (sometimes colloquially referred to as Y-chromosomal Adam and mitochondrial Eve). Students learn that humans' common ancestors were from Africa (likely the Great Rift Valley), possibly lived during similar times—but were not mates—and had the ability to make tools, build a fire, and communicate. After students examine one set of scientific explanations, they then learn the human origin stories from numerous groups around the world, including the Haudenosaunee (Iroquois), Mayan, Māori, Egyptian, Roman, Hindu, Chinese, Yoruba, and Abrahamic (Jewish, Christian, and Muslim) peoples. For instance, many students find similarities between the scientific explanation of Pangaea and part of the Haudenosaunee explanation of Turtle Island. At the end of the unit, students are asked to write their own interpretations of the world and humans' origin. They are encouraged to choose the explanation that is most compelling to them or combine multiple explanations. For instance, some Christian students may choose an intelligent design view that combines the Genesis account with scientific evidence.

In the last mini-unit, Ms. Smith helps the students examine the beginning of distinct human cultures. They study human migration and how people moved throughout the world. The students then study the early peoples in Africa, Asia, Europe, and the Americas and how the environment impacted their cultures, including their physical appearances, ways of life, languages, and religions. Ms. Smith had recently read Dunbar-Ortiz's (2015) work on the Native peoples of the Americas, where the author made the argument that Indigenous people in the Americas had the same level of sophistication in agriculture as people on other continents at that time. Ms. Smith has students compare and contrast early agricultural societies, including making arguments about whether the domestication of animals, which was common in Europe, Africa, and Asia, was a better strategy than game management, which was common in the Americas. She also has them examine the different types of plants that were domesticated on each continent and consider ways that certain foods may have had an influence on developing cultures. She also has the students examine different ancient societies' views of the land as private property or communal resources. She has them examine several matriarchal societies in the ancient world, including Kush Queendoms, Sitones of Northern Europe, Hopi, and Na (Mosuo) in modern-day China. Students examine the female kin system and matriarchal communal societies common among the Indigenous peoples of the Americas

(Dunbar-Ortiz, 2015). She has them read and debate an article that claims sexism started over 12,000 years ago, when humans moved to a homesteading and agriculture-based society. Before that time, anthropologists have argued that there was significant gender egalitarianism, and women were involved in communal decisionmaking (Ananthaswamy & Douglas, 2018; Dyble et al., 2015).

In the last part of the unit, students engage in a comparative study of world religions. Despite being a devout Christian, Ms. Smith worries that Christianity is often taught as "facts," where other religions are taught as "stories." To help students see their Christian-centric perspective on world religions, Ms. Smith creates classroom activities that ask them to study Christianity as outsiders, but they will later share how they felt when their religion was depicted that way. In a predominantly Christian space, Ms. Smith's students push back on the idea that other religions had valid beliefs. Instead of discounting her students' religious views, she uses their strong faith backgrounds to help them gain a better awareness of their Christian-centric beliefs. While it does not change most students' beliefs, it helps them understand people different than themselves and realize that it is important to stand up for the religious rights and freedoms of all people. Ms. Smith connects their studies of world religions to current events involving religious discrimination across the world, including in the United States.

Unit 2: Ancient Africa. Once students have learned about the origin of humans, Ms. Smith has them study ancient Africa, and specifically the Nok people and the kingdoms of Ghana, Mali, and Songhay. She intentionally chooses ancient peoples from across the continent to highlight the cultural differences. Ms. Smith launches this study by playing the song "I Can" by the rapper Nas, and she has the students analyze the lyrics, which include the following lines:

> Be, be-fore we came to this country
> We were kings and queens, never porch monkeys
> There was empires in Africa called Kush
> Timbuktu, where every race came to get books
> To learn from black teachers who taught Greeks and Romans
> Asian, Arabs and gave them gold, when
> Gold was converted to money it all changed
> Money then became empowerment for Europeans
> The Persian military invaded
> They heard about the gold, the teachings, and everything sacred
> Africa was almost robbed naked
> Slavery was money, so they began making slave ships
> Egypt was the place that Alexander the Great went
> He was so shocked at the mountains with black faces

Shot up they nose to impose what basically
Still goes on today, you see?
If the truth is told, the youth can grow
They'll learn to survive until they gain control. (Nas, 2003)

Ms. Smith helps students unpack some of the anti-racist ideas in the song, including how the idea of comparing African people to monkeys or other animals began in ancient Greece and Rome (Isaac, 2004). Students have the opportunity to make the connection between these lyrics and the way they have been taught history in the past. Ms. Smith then spends time having them explore the accomplishments and achievements of the West African kingdoms prior to colonization. A key goal here is that students will understand the notion that Black history began long before the transatlantic slave trade, which is not the way Black history is frequently taught in our schools. In fact, Ms. Smith ends this exploration with the discussion question, "Why is this history of thriving African civilizations often *not* taught in our schools?" This gives students the chance to share their thinking on the choices that are made in the teaching of history and whose perspectives drive those choices.

Unit 3: Ancient Asia. In the third unit, Ms. Smith has the students shift to a study of ancient Asia, and specifically ancient Mesopotamia, China, and India. Students learn of the vast empires that existed in each region. They learn about the peoples' understandings of science, creation of artwork and architecture, and religious beliefs. They compare and contrast the different societies and political structures, including the social classes of Mesopotamia, the Confucian social structures of China, and the four *varnas* of India. At the end of the unit, Ms. Smith wants the students to connect the characteristics of these ancient civilizations to their own lives. The students are assigned a civilization and are asked to describe at least five characteristics that show how that society cared for its people. Ms. Smith then asks them to compare the services created by that civilization to those that are present in the city of Charleston. The students must explain the importance of each service and how ordinary people, not always powerful individuals, were responsible for the collective care of their fellow humans.

Unit 4: Ancient Americas. In the next unit, Ms. Smith has the students examine the ancient peoples of their own continent. Often, Indigenous people from the Americas are left out from studies of ancient history. This omission may imply that Indigenous people were not from civilizations and were not equal to the people in Europe, Africa, or Asia.

The students start the unit with a debate over the possible migration routes that Indigenous people may have taken to arrive in the Americas.

Using anthropological and historical evidence, they have to build a case as to which possible theory—over land or over sea—may be more likely. Next, they engage in a study of several different groups of Indigenous peoples from the American continent. They start with the Salish peoples of the Pacific Northwest. Students learn about their early way of life through a digital exploration of the Marpole Midden National Historic Site in British Columbia, which is a village and burial site dating back to 2,000 BCE. They also learn how this Native gravesite was disturbed by archaeologists in the 1890s, and how most of it was destroyed to build a hotel in the 1950s. The students learn about the Salish language and culture, including the differences between coastal and inland groups, and the cultural influence on the region today. As with each Indigenous nation studied, Ms. Smith has the students link the people's ancient history to current events by having them examine current event issues that impact each group today. For instance, when they study the Salish peoples, Ms. Smith has students look up current events related to various Indigenous groups in the Pacific Northwest today. They report on what they have learned from various articles, such as a cell phone application that is being used to sustain the Salishan languages today, an annual bitterroot harvest, and a dam project on the Flathead Indian Reservation.

Next, the students study the Maya people. To help them understand that groups that are described as a collective group today were often distinct, culturally separate groups in the past, Ms. Smith assigns groups of students in her class to research the ancient history of particular regions where today's Maya people historically lived, including modern-day Yucatán, Chiapas, Tabasco, El Salvador, Honduras, Belize, and Guatemala. They learn about the invention of the Maya calendar, mathematics and science, artwork and architecture, and religious beliefs. The students then study the Mississippian people and the ancient city of Cahokia. They take a virtual field trip to the Cahokia Mounds Museum to examine a civilization larger than most of Europe at the time. Students learn about the elaborate social and agricultural systems of the region, as well as the vast network of trade in the area, which linked Cahokia to much of North America. In the final series of lessons, the students examine the Indigenous peoples of West Virginia and the archaeological evidence of their communities that date back thousands of years. They also learn about the Indigenous peoples' relationships to the modern nations of the Shawnee, Delaware, Cherokee, and Seneca peoples.

Unit 5: Ancient Europe. In the final unit, Ms. Smith has the students study the peoples of ancient Europe, specifically those of ancient Greece and Rome, as well as the Goths and Huns. Ms. Smith wants students to understand that the people of ancient Greece were not one group and that they did not have one unified nation or government. She wants to highlight the stories of regular people of this region and teach the nuances of the nondominant group. The people known as the "ancient Greeks" were different groups, and each group had its own small communities due to the terrain that separated them. Communities developed independently of one another and eventually formed self-governing city-states; as many as 1,500 ancient Greek city-states existed, and many had their own practices, rituals, and rivalries. Ms. Smith asks her students to become anthropologists and investigate a community of ancient Greeks. She then asks them to write an article using the Nacirema example studied in the beginning of the year to describe the practices, rituals, and rivalries of their assigned community. She wants the students to pay particular attention to how something strange or foreign to one group may be natural to another. For these investigations, Ms. Smith encourages them to highlight ordinary people and their contributions, rather than highlight the leaders, to demonstrate the work of regular people in these regions.

Field Experiences and Classroom Guests

Ancient history can be particularly hard for middle school students to understand, as it is far removed from our present-day way of life. As such, Ms. Smith knows that it is important to take her students on multiple field experiences. This can be particularly difficult, as many historical sites are hours away from Charleston. However, she takes students on two field trips during the year. In the fall, when they are learning about ancient Africa and Asia, Ms. Smith organizes a 7th-grade overnight field trip to Washington, D.C. Students visit the Smithsonian Institution and participate in an ancient art and culture study there. They work with a museum curator and have a chance to learn about ancient African and Asian cultures through a study of their cultural artifacts. In the spring, when students are studying the ancient peoples of the eastern United States, Ms. Smith takes them on a field trip to the Delf Norona Museum in Moundsville, West Virginia, where they research the history of the 2,000-year-old mound and burial grounds. This field trip is especially important for her students, as there are multiple burial mounds within the city limits of Charleston but none are fully contextualized, and many students have walked by the mounds, or played on them, without knowing their history. After the field trip, Ms. Smith has students visit similar mounds in their own school's neighborhood. This turns into a community-based project where groups of students research the Adena people, who built the mounds. Each group then records a brief podcast about different aspects of the Adena people and their society. They then post the podcasts on the school's website and post signs with QR codes and embedded videos around the neighborhood to educate fellow community members about the Native peoples whose land they are on.

Ms. Smith also knows the importance of students connecting the past to the present. Since much of their studies involve ancient African people,

Ms. Smith creates a digital friendship with a middle school in Cape Town, South Africa. Each month, Ms. Smith has her students video conference with the students and teachers there. They educate each other about the ancient people of their respective homes, but they also learn about their cultural, social, and political similarities and differences today.

Finally, Ms. Smith brings in multiple guest speakers over the course of the year to enhance the learning that is happening in the classroom. Representatives from the local synagogue, mosque, and Hindu temple visit the classroom to speak during the students' study of those religions. Students in the archaeology program at Marshall University in Huntington, West Virginia, also visit the classroom to speak with students about their work, as well as discuss the careers they could seek upon graduating that might help preserve and sustain different cultures and histories.

Assessment

Ms. Smith knows that there are many ways that students can demonstrate their knowledge and understanding of the past. She is particularly interested in having them engage in larger projects that demonstrate their academic skills, while also supporting them in what can be larger and more challenging tasks. At the end of each unit, she has students work individually or in groups to answer significant questions related to justice and fairness in the past, often connecting it to the present. Through group presentations or individual reports, students are asked the following questions about the people that they have studied throughout the year:

- Did a group of people at the time want to change society, and did they have a vision for how it might look different? If so, what was that vision and how was it different?
- Did a group of people at the time outline and help educate the public about a particular type of oppression and the ways that they could work against it? Did they make the case to the public that alternatives to the status quo would benefit all?
- Did a group of people at the time engage in collective actions? (Was there a "trigger event" that gained public attention? What methods were used to raise public awareness?) Did the movement gain public support? Did the group's collective actions lead to a change in society? Is there still a legacy of this today?

Ms. Smith knows the importance of making these summative assessments relevant and exciting to the students. For instance, at the end of the ancient Africa unit, they are asked to create a graphic novel of one of the studied African empires, where they must answer all of the required end-of-unit questions. It is an opportunity for students to present their knowledge in a way that is captivating and engaging; it connects to forms of popular culture that they may regularly interact with.

At the end of the year, Ms. Smith has the students take all of their accumulated understandings of ancient civilizations and work in groups to create their ideal ancient society. At the core of this project, the students must decide which ancient conceptions of justice they found most compelling, and then they must design their society's health care and practices, trade, religion, government, and social structures.

REFLECTION QUESTIONS

1. What are the strongest justice-oriented aspects of Ms. Smith's classroom? How might you adapt these techniques for your students?
2. How are the principles of equity and justice apparent inside and outside of Ms. Smith's history classroom? What other justice-oriented components would you add to her classroom?
3. What are some potential barriers or pitfalls in using social inquiry with middle school students? How might teachers overcome those?
4. How does Ms. Smith integrate the other aspects of social studies (i.e., civics, geography, economics) in her history classroom? How can teachers support justice-oriented social studies instruction?
5. How can field experiences and classroom guests contribute to the preparation of middle school students as engaged citizens and activists? Have you designed any of these experiences for your students?

CHAPTER 9

State and Local History at the Elementary Level

Mr. Frank Hashimoto

With Jennifer R. Bryson, Boston University

We often underestimate younger children's ability to understand the past. We also undervalue the sophistication with which they can consider issues of fairness and justice. Children are naturally inquisitive learners who are continually making sense of the world (Donaldson, 1979; Levstik & Barton, 2011). One of the subjects that children, including young children, know best is people (Levstik & Barton, 2011). They spend most of their days learning through their interactions with other people as they begin to develop a sense of community. They are continually thinking about themselves in relation to their families, cities and towns, nations, and world. Moreover, children can reason about the beliefs and intentions of others (Donaldson, 1979; Levstik & Barton, 2011), and they have strong understandings of fairness (Wade, 2007). As Levstik and Barton argued (2011), these are similar to the skills that historians use to understand the past, where they "focus on the human sense of situations; much of their work involves studying the beliefs and intentions of people in the past" (p. 15). As such, teachers, and especially elementary teachers, should focus on the human elements of the past. They should expose younger students to the choices made by people in the past and help them see that people had (and still have) conflicting views of historical events.

As young as preschool and kindergarten, students are also making sense of race, gender, class, and linguistic differences (Bolgatz, 2005; Brown & Brown, 2011; Epstein, 2009; Levstik & Barton, 2011; Quintana, 1998; Ramsey, 1991; Shutts, 2015; Tatum, 1997; Theimer et al., 2001; Wade, 2007). They are noticing differences between themselves and others in physical appearance, culture, language, and social practices. Additionally, young children also begin to recognize that unfairness and discrimination can relate to race, gender, class, and ability (Bolgatz, 2005; Epstein, 2009; Quintana, 1998; Tatum, 1997; Theimer et al., 2001; Wade, 2007).

It is important that younger students have frequent opportunities to engage in sense-making related to the discipline of history and issues of justice. Similar to how Becker (1932) viewed every person as their own historian, using history to help make judgments and interpretations in their present world, we argue that young children must also learn to be their own historians. They should be given opportunities to interpret the meaning of past events, as it helps them understand their present world. Elementary-age students should be questioning if people made right or wrong decisions in the past, and they should gain an understanding for how history helped create the world that they currently live in. Moreover, we contend that younger students should have opportunities to be activists for causes that are important for them. Teachers can provide time in their daily schedules for students to think about their values (and those of their families) and to consider ways to solve our current world problems (most of which are rooted in those past decisions). This is the opportune time to develop their civic-mindedness around issues that they care about, as elementary school is where students often start to find their passions and develop their moral beliefs.

We have spent countless hours in elementary classrooms where we have seen students wondering about issues of immigration, the environment, racism, sexism, hunger, and poverty. Unfortunately, despite having an ability to ask questions about the past and present world, elementary students are rarely asked to engage in inquiry or to investigate questions of meaning in the classroom (Levstik & Barton, 2011). The most common types of elementary history instruction include storytelling and the completion of fact-recall worksheets (Bailey et al., 2006; Levstik & Barton, 2011; VanSledright & Brophy, 1992), if students receive history instruction at all—as there has been a decline in history education at the elementary level (Bailey et al., 2006; Ellington et al., 2006; Fitchett & Heafner, 2010; Fitchett, Heafner, & Lambert, 2014a, 2014b; Fitchett, Heafner, & VanFossen, 2014; Heafner & Fitchett, 2012a, 2012b).

We argue that by focusing the study of history on justice within the elementary classroom, students will gain an important foundation in their learning. If history learning does not focus on equity and fairness at an early age, then we have found that middle and high school students are often stunted in their justice-oriented thinking. Moreover, we have heard countless older students (at the secondary or university level) say that they cannot understand why their elementary-level history only focused on the "good stories" of the past or one group's version. They are surprised to learn that certain events were not taught with accuracy or truthfulness for the sake of not potentially hurting their feelings (Columbus's interactions with the Arawak and the Pilgrims' interactions with the Wampanoag are two examples of this). While it was not their teachers' intentions, students often feel robbed of the real history and are confused why they did not learn the truth about these events until later in their educational careers. Of course, their teachers may have been guided by a false sense that the younger students were not ready to learn about difficult histories, or they felt topics related to inequity and injustice were taboo or inappropriate for younger children (Evans et al., 1999; Husband, 2010; James, 2008) or their multiethnic content knowledge was not strong enough to field questions about multicultural or difficult histories (Branch, 2004; Brown & Brown, 2011). Yet there is evidence that when approached in an appropriate way, students can be empowered by learning about the ways that people worked to overcome injustice and unfairness (Epstein, 2009; Husband, 2010; Levstik & Barton, 2011; Wade, 2007).

By focusing the study of history on justice, it also helps better prepare elementary students to become engaged citizens. Moreover, in an increasingly diverse nation and world, citizens must develop the key skills of perspective-taking, understanding cultural differences, and considering the needs of all members of society (Banks, 2004). Elementary history classrooms should foster what Westheimer and Kahne (2004) called justice-oriented citizens, or citizens who consider the root causes of civics problems and think about ways to make society more equitable (Westheimer, 2015). Starting in preschool and the primary grades, students learn how to participate in a democracy and begin to contribute ideas as to how society can be improved (Serriere, 2019). Teachers can use the study of history to encourage students to act on one another's behalf within communities and to ask questions about fairness in the larger society. This is especially important for students to develop in their early years, as there is evidence that exposure to high-quality civics in elementary school influences civic participation later in life (Kahne & Middaugh, 2008; LeCompte et al., in press). We also suspect that when students practice engaging in activism, participating in movements, and advocating for causes of personal importance, it may support these types of civic actions later in life. It will help them understand that the common narrative of how the single individual can change society is inaccurate and unhelpful; instead, we must work together to bring about change.

HISTORY FOR JUSTICE IN THE STATE AND LOCAL HISTORY CLASSROOM

Elementary school is the time when students first engage in a serious study of the past. It is when they not only begin to understand the differences between past and present, but also practice taking moral stances about the past (Levstik & Barton, 2011). Before middle school, students are also beginning to develop their disciplinary identities and affinities for certain school subjects, including history (Carlone et al., 2014; Cvencek et al., 2011; Hill et al., 2018; Kim, 2018; Mayes et al., 2016; Parker, 2008; Varelas et al., 2012). It is often when students start to believe that they are "good at" history or decide that history is their favorite subject. There is evidence that younger students' disciplinary identities intersect with their racial, gender, and class identities (Carlone et al., 2014; Kane, 2012; Varelas et al., 2012). While the structural racism and sexism embedded in our society often deters students of color or girls from seeing themselves as having aptitude in science or mathematics (Carlone et al., 2014; Kane, 2012; Varelas et al., 2012), this manifests differently in history. Instead, students of color and girls often learn starting in the elementary grades that history is not relevant to their lives, since it does not seem to include their lived experiences (Brown & Brown, 2011; Brugar et al., 2014; Busey & Walker, 2017; Hahn et al., 2007). Many students, especially those from nondominant groups, do not see their histories in the elementary curriculum (Bolgatz, 2005; Hawkman, 2018). If they do see themselves in lesson materials or textbooks, they are often a side story (e.g., Sacagawea, Harriet Tubman, Dolores Huerta), or they are literally placed in the sidebar (as so many textbooks place people of color and women there). Moreover, when they do see themselves or their ancestors in the curriculum, it is often void of resistance, activism, and intellectual agency; the elementary history curriculum has generally focused on individual acts of patriotism as opposed to collective resistance (Busey & Walker, 2017). Like secondary history education, elementary students often learn about important individuals (e.g., Martin Luther King Jr., Rosa Parks, César Chávez), rather than larger movements of social change. The elementary curriculum typically presents certain groups as victims (i.e., Black people during slavery or segregation, Indigenous people during European colonization), rather than groups engaged in a struggle against oppressors or advancing their own societies. It may leave students, especially from oppressed social groups, with the belief that their histories are unimportant or an insignificant component of the larger historical narrative of a nation or world. Or worse, their freedom was the result of members of the dominant group (e.g., Whites, men, the wealthy, straight people) giving it to them. To remedy this, starting from an early age, students should confront issues of race, racism, and social justice more broadly (Brown & Brown, 2011). Additionally, they should have regular opportunities to examine the role of gender, class, sexual orientation, and immigration status in the past. As such, we argue that history for justice must begin in the primary grades, so it can lay a foundation for students' later historical learning. The primary grades are the opportune time to engage them in historical inquiry and to introduce an analysis of the past that focuses on fairness and equity. This will not only have an impact on students' understanding of the past, but also potentially help foster their own positive social identities (An, 2020; Epstein, 2009; Jones et al., 2001; Levstik & Barton, 2011).

In this chapter, we present a vignette that illustrates what teaching history for justice can look like in an elementary classroom that is focused on state and local history. We attempt to illustrate how teachers can help elementary students analyze the past by considering moments of unfairness and injustice. Like the previous chapters on middle and high school teachers, this chapter emphasizes the ways that elementary-level history should center on activism and movement building, rather than teaching about individual heroes (which is commonly the focus of elementary history curriculum). It also provides examples of what social inquiry, critical multiculturalism, and transformative democratic citizenship look like at the elementary level. While the teacher is imagined, he is an amalgamation of practices that we have learned from the numerous elementary generalist teachers and other teachers we have researched over the past decade (Martell, 2017, 2018; Martell & Stevens, 2017a, 2017b; Martell & Stevens, 2019), or they were practices that we used ourselves as classroom teachers. We hope this chapter offers ways that elementary teachers may reinvent their history classrooms. We start at the beginning of the school year and follow the teacher and students until the end of the school year.

MR. HASHIMOTO'S ELEMENTARY SCHOOL STATE AND LOCAL HISTORY CLASSROOM

Mr. Frank Hashimoto grew up in San Francisco, California, where he attended public schools that were racially and economically diverse. He is Japanese American and his parents were Nisei, or the first generation born in the United States. During World War II, his parents and grandparents were incarcerated at the Tule Lake Segregation Center, a Japanese American concentration camp in Newell, California. They were what is referred to by some in the Japanese American community as "no-no boys" and "no-no girls," which were incarcerated people who refused to answer yes on two questions in a loyalty questionnaire administered by the U.S. government. Their objection was a political action to protest their imprisonment and the violations of their rights. As a young child, Mr. Hashimoto often heard his parents and grandparents refer to "camp," and many of his views of race and justice are rooted in his family's experiences before, during, and after World War II, where they faced numerous acts of discrimination and racism. He heard his grandparents tell numerous stories of not being able to rent houses in the White neighborhoods of the Bay Area or be seated at restaurants that refused to serve Asian Americans.

Growing up in San Francisco, Mr. Hashimoto had many experiences interacting with friends and peers from different racial and ethnic backgrounds. His mother and father were teachers, and from an early age, he also wanted to be a teacher. After high school, he graduated from a local private university with a degree in psychology and then attended a local state university to receive his teaching credential. After he earned his credential, he accepted a job teaching 1st grade at the same elementary school that he attended as a child. Mr. Hashimoto is now in his 15th year as a teacher; he teaches 4th grade (he moved grades in his third year), which includes a history curriculum on the state and local histories of California.

Mr. Hashimoto is also the leader of his school's equity action team, which involves professional development, support for colleagues, and group meetings around issues of equity in the school. This teacher-led group meets once per month to have conversations about race and develop equitable teaching practices. The group strives to create a climate where students of color feel valued and see themselves in the curriculum. Most recently, they developed lists of read-aloud books with authentic representations of multicultural characters and discussion guides for each grade level, being careful to avoid what Rodríguez (in press-a, in press-b) called deeply problematic depictions of race (which are common in many books highlighting social activism or civil rights). Mr. Hashimoto is instrumental in supporting his colleagues as they challenge each other to build diverse classroom libraries, where all students are able to see themselves represented in the classroom texts. The equity action team frequently presents at faculty meetings and during full-day professional development days. His colleagues have commented on the integral role that this group plays in providing support and professional development to all teachers as they develop equitable curricula and practices.

Classroom Culture

Before the school year begins, Mr. Hashimoto schedules in-person meetings, phone calls, texts, or emails (depending on what format works best) with his students' parents, where he asks them about their children's needs and their home cultures and languages. Mr. Hashimoto speaks English, Japanese, and Spanish, but he often has to rely on district translation services to connect with parents who speak other languages. Getting to know the parents and students before the start of school helps Mr. Hashimoto create a classroom that acknowledges the students' differences and enables him to create culturally relevant and sustaining lessons throughout the year.

In the classroom, Mr. Hashimoto has students work in grouped desks, and he often uses a diverse array of activities each day. By the second or third week of school, the students are used to collaborating in groups, problem solving, grappling with difficult questions, and sharing their ideas on academically challenging tasks during their social studies time (as well as in other subject areas). Mr. Hashimoto also knows it is important to give students chances to be leaders among their peers. Each student has different classroom responsibilities that rotate every week. This includes organizational roles, such as paper passer or cubby manager, and it also includes roles that ask them to be responsible for each other, such as classmate listener (students who keep an eye out for, and inform the teacher of, any classmates who may need help or are having a difficult day) and recess buddy (students who make sure that everyone is included in lunch or recess group activities). Mr. Hashimoto often refers to the class as a team, and he discusses how each of the students plays a very important role in how the classroom operates. He begins the year by sharing with them that they each have the right to an education, a right to be treated with kindness, and a right to a fair classroom. The responsibilities shared among the students represent more than classroom jobs—they are the students' contributions to the team.

Not all of the elementary schools in the district include dedicated time for teaching social studies. Therefore, during Mr. Hashimoto's first few years as a classroom teacher, he worked with the principal to establish two to three periods each week for social studies at their school. They also created end-of-the-year social studies projects that had students use their knowledge in history, geography, civics, and economics, as well as literacy and math skills, on monthlong interdisciplinary projects that were shared with the community. Through a 4th-grade history fair, students present a different aspect of San Francisco's past, from the first Indigenous people to today. He encourages students to choose topics that interest them and connect to their social identities. Mr. Hashimoto wants the community to be involved in the classroom, so during the history fair he invites people from the neighborhood to visit and dialogue with students about their projects.

Pedagogical Approaches

While Mr. Hashimoto uses many different pedagogical techniques in his classroom, his pedagogy is most aligned with what Martell (2018) described as *discovering*, "where a teacher views the role as presenting different cultural perspectives of the past or present and then allows the students to make interpretations" (p. 69). He aims to help them "understand their own identities and cultures, while also encouraging students to view the content of social studies as composed of many competing, diverse perspectives" (Martell & Stevens, 2019, p. 6). He often asks students if they think something in the past or present is fair, and he then helps them brainstorm ways to make it fairer. He values inquiry-based instruction and knows that students can make historical arguments before 4th grade. Many of his lessons have them use adapted primary and secondary sources to debate, discuss, and make sense of the past. He also helps his students learn to ask and answer their own historical questions. When he starts a new unit, he uses a KWL chart to solicit from his students their curiosities (where they capture what they know, what to know, and later, what they have learned) and to activate their prior knowledge. Mr. Hashimoto also has students engage in real-world civics opportunities. For example, during the unit on the California mission system, he incorporates sources showing the perspectives of various oppressed groups in the Spanish colonies, including women,

Indigenous peoples, enslaved people, and children. The students noticed that these groups were not included in the textbook, which they sometimes use in class as a reference book. Rather, the textbook's chapter on the mission system was written from the Spanish missionaries' perspectives. As a culminating assignment, the students wrote a letter to the publishing company demanding that it include more perspectives of these groups in the textbook. After a few months, the class received a reply letter from a representative at the book company. This gave the students an opportunity to see how their civic voice can be used to make the history texts more just; it allowed them to practice activism.

Curriculum

Mr. Hashimoto finds strategic ways to use the state-mandated history curriculum to teach history for justice. In California, 4th grade is state and local history, and Mr. Hashimoto uses this content to help his students see a long history of unfairness in their community and that many of their community members have organized over time for justice. In the first days of school, he has students discuss their own definitions of fairness and justice, and he asks them to think of people they know or characters they have read about that have faced injustice. This occurs not only during social studies time, but also during literacy blocks (a place where he chooses to expand students' exposure to history content). For example, in a literacy unit on sports, Mr. Hashimoto selects readings on athletes of color across history, including texts like *Teammates* by Peter Golenbock and Paul Bacon (1992), *Just Like Josh Gibson* by Angela Johnson and Beth Peck (2007), *Jim Thorpe's Bright Path* by Joseph Bruchac and S. D. Nelson (2008), *Baseball Saved Us* by Ken Mochizuki and Dom Lee (2009), *Emmanuel's Dream: The True Story of Emmanuel Ofosu Yeboah* by Laurie Ann Thompson and Sean Qualls (2015), and *Pelé, King of Soccer/El Rey del Fútbol* by Monica Brown and Rudy Gutierrez (2017). Throughout the unit, Mr. Hashimoto uses the history of sports to discuss the themes of fairness and justice within the texts.

Unit 1: Indigenous Peoples of the Bay Area. The first social studies unit that Mr. Hashimoto teaches is about the First Nations of California, with a specific focus on the Ohlone, Miwok, and Pomo, who are the Indigenous peoples of the Bay Area. In one lesson, he has students engage in an activity where there are stations throughout the classroom representing different Native groups in the Bay Area. Each station has a large bag; the students go around the room and pull out items from the large bags to examine the political, social, and economic components of each early Native society. For example, Pomo women became internationally known for their basket-weaving techniques, so when the students go to that station, they pull out a small basket with historical information. Miwok people played mixed-gender games on a large playing field called *poscoi a we'a*, so this station includes an image of the field and a ball and an explanation of the gender-inclusive rules. At the Ohlone station, students examine a model of the traditional dome-shaped houses with information on how they were built. They then use the information that they collected from the stations, along with information from the Native nations' websites, to edit and revise the historical accuracy of the simple English Wikipedia pages for each Indigenous nation. Students then share their pages through a gallery walk presentation. In the subsequent days, they participate in lessons on the peoples' traditional ways of life, languages, and histories. The unit ends looking at current events that relate to these Indigenous groups today, including issues of sovereignty, a project to clean a lake on the nearby Pomo reservation, and participation by local Native activists in the Dakota Access Pipeline protests.

Unit 2: Arrival of the Spanish Outsiders. Once the students have learned about the people who first lived in the Bay Area, they are ready to learn about the upheaval that was first caused by Spanish settlers and later caused by American settlers in the Bay Area. Mr. Hashimoto's second unit focuses on the invasion of outsiders and their related colonization. It begins with a critical examination of the California mission system. Most elementary students in California learn about the 21 Spanish religious missions established in the 18th and 19th centuries to Christianize the Indigenous people, and about Padre Junípero Serra, who was an early leader of the missions and is usually depicted as a hero. The unit begins with a lesson called "Whose Maps?" that has students engage in a critical reading of Mission-era California maps. Students answer the question: "Who/what is shown in early maps of Mission-era California, and who/what is left out? Why did cartographers make these choices?" Traditionally, students often write and share reports on each mission. Mr. Hashimoto does the same, but instead of presenting the missions from the Spanish perspective, he asks students to present from the Native peoples' perspective. They learn about the forced Christianization and violence used on the Native people; for instance, each mission had a whipping post, usually in the middle of the plaza (Dunbar-Ortiz, 2015). The unit continues with the Mexican War of Independence and how that impacted the people of California. Students are asked to take on the role of numerous Indigenous people or Californios (Mexicans born in California) and journal about the various events and how they affected their lives. This allows them to understand the diverse and complex perspectives of the people living in California at the time.

Unit 3: The United States Takes California. Next, the students prepare and engage in a debate on the U.S.-Mexico War/Intervención Estadounidense en México from the American and Mexican perspectives. They have to answer the question, "Was the U.S. government justified in its invasion of Mexico?"

The unit ends with California going from U.S. territory to state. It involves a simulation of the California Gold Rush, where students are asked to take on the roles of different groups (i.e., Anglos, Californios, Black Freemen, Pomo and Yalesummi, and Chinese people), and they have to abide by certain rules during a classroom gold hunt. The rules simulate the constraints of the racial caste laws of the time (e.g., Californios and Chinese and Native people not being allowed to own land or vote and being required to pay higher taxes on the gold they found). In the debrief, students are able to describe how official citizenship gave White Americans advantages over the other groups, despite the fact that Californios and the Indigenous peoples had lived on the land for much longer. They also highlight the disadvantages that Chinese people and Black freemen faced due to their race. By studying the California Gold Rush, students are better able to see why the Compromise of 1850 was incredibly important as it established California as a free state, but it also continued to maintain and expand the system of slavery that existed in other parts of the United States.

Unit 4: Bridging California and the World. Throughout the year, Mr. Hashimoto continues to teach local history from a justice-oriented perspective. He teaches about the Civil War through the lens of California's soldiers. When he covers the transcontinental railroad, he centers the students' studies on the Chinese and Irish immigrants who built the railroad. California as a home for immigrants is a common thread throughout his class. Mr. Hashimoto has students learn about the Angel Island Immigration Station through a schoolwide scavenger hunt. Each student receives directions for where they should go in the school to learn about the experiences of Asian immigrants disembarking in San Francisco. At the school nurse's office, he gives students a history lesson on how immigrants had forced medical quarantines. At the main office, he has them answer a real immigration questionnaire from Angel Island. In his own classroom, Mr. Hashimoto shows a video of interviews with Chinese, Japanese, and Indian people who immigrated through Angel Island. He discusses with students how many Asians were forced to return to their home countries due to the Chinese Exclusion Act and the Immigration Act of 1924, while others were denied citizenship through court cases and not allowed to own land as the result of laws. At the gym, students experience a replica of one of the large halls where immigrants stayed; the replica has the correct dimensions taped on the floor with cots set up representing the bunks. At the end of the activity, the students return to their classroom where they have to write a letter to their relatives back home in China, Japan, or India explaining what it was like to be at Angel Island. Mr. Hashimoto hopes to teach the students historical empathy skills and help them gain a deeper understanding of the injustice of the immigration system at the time. At the same time, he is very careful to not have them participate in any simulations of historical violence or discrimination. He ends this unit asking students the question from the California state standards: "Why did people migrate despite all the hardships they faced?" The students participate in a Socratic seminar, answering that question with a newfound and deeper understanding for the immigrant experience.

Unit 5: California and Civil Rights. Throughout the year, the students continue to learn history through the nondominant group lenses. They study various topics that highlight the struggle for justice that happened in California: the Tule Lake Segregation Center, Fred Korematsu's resistance to incarceration during World War II, the *Mendez v. Westminster* segregation case, the United Farm Workers movement, the passage of the Immigration and Nationality Act of 1965 and new groups arriving in California, the formation of the Black Panthers in Oakland, the American Indian Movement's Occupation of Alcatraz, the activism of the Third World Liberation Front, the election of Harvey Milk, the right of gay men and lesbians to teach and later marry in California, and the organization of Justice for Vincent Chin protests in San Francisco. The last lesson focuses on the use of sweatshop and child labor in California and around the world. The students participate in an activity called "Our Clothes Have Stories Too," with the inquiry question, "Where do our clothes come from and who makes them?" Students look at where their clothes are from and then research the labor practices of that country using primary and secondary sources provided by Mr. Hashimoto. After they document the injustices of child and sweatshop labor, the students then work in teams to create child labor laws that would protect child laborers.

Field Experiences and Classroom Guests

Mr. Hashimoto knows how important it is that his students meet people who have experienced injustice in the past, and he also knows that they need opportunities to learn about movements for change in their communities. He routinely has guest speakers visit his classroom, and he takes his students on multiple field trips each year. At the beginning of the year, the students experience an interdisciplinary unit on fairness and justice. Across literacy, social studies, and science, they investigate different moments in the past and present where people advocated for change. During the unit, Mr. Hashimoto has his students read the book *The Bracelet* (Uchida & Yardley, 1996) that tells the story of a girl who is sent to a Japanese American World War II concentration camp. He has his parents visit the classroom and share their experiences as children being incarcerated there. These activities help prepare his students for a year where they will continuously ask, "Was everyone treated fairly in California? What did people do when there was injustice?" Students are incredibly engaged speaking to people who are the same age as Emi, the main character of the book. They ask thoughtful questions about fairness and justice. Mr. Hashimoto's parents bring pictures from their childhood (including one that was taken on their last day in camp). During the first social studies unit, Mr. Hashimoto takes the students on a field trip to the Museum of the American Indian in Novato, California, which is the site of a Coast Miwok village. There they learn about the Native peoples of the Bay Area from a member of the Federated Indians of Graton Rancheria, and on the following Saturday the students' families attend the Trade Feast on the site with Mr. Hashimoto. The event includes Native arts and crafts, drumming, dancing, songs, stories, shell bead drilling, basketry demonstrations, and tours of the museum. It is a chance for the students to gain a deeper understanding of Indigenous people in the present and connect it to the study of the past.

Assessment

The last unit of the year focuses on California in the 20th century. Mr. Hashimoto has the students revisit some of the issues that they studied in past lessons, such as the treatment of Indigenous people and immigrants and the creation of labor laws. They also learn about new issues impacting California, such as climate change, dis/ability rights, and unfair funding of school districts. Mr. Hashimoto assigns students an issue based on the particular issues that interest them. The students research their issue and create a presentation. He encourages them to use whatever form of presentation is most compelling to them. Some choose to write poems, create a newspaper, write and perform a song, or create a wall mural. The class shares their presentations with an audience of parents during a publishing party.

REFLECTION QUESTIONS

1. What are the strongest justice-oriented aspects of Mr. Hashimoto's classroom? How might you adapt these techniques for your students?
2. How are the principles of equity and justice apparent inside and outside of Mr. Hashimoto's social studies block? What other justice-oriented components would you add to his classroom?
3. What are some potential barriers or pitfalls in using social inquiry with elementary students? How might teachers overcome those?
4. How does Mr. Hashimoto integrate social studies with literacy instruction? How can teachers support justice-oriented social studies-based literacy instruction?
5. How can field experiences and classroom guests contribute to the preparation of elementary students as engaged citizens and activists? Have you designed any of these experiences for your students?

CHAPTER 10

Overcoming Barriers

Oppression is interwoven into our histories. Yet the study of history offers potential tools for deconstructing past oppression. When history education is centered on the narratives of dominant social groups and the actions of powerful individuals, it maintains the status quo and often masks the existence of oppressive systems by making people believe that the world is and always was supposed to be this way. Inequity is inevitable and justice for all is impossible. When history education is centered on the narratives of nondominant groups and the actions of activists and movements, it helps people understand how we arrived at the inequitable present; instead, the status quo was not predetermined, and together we can build more equitable and just societies (as many have already been working toward this goal). Equity becomes inevitable if justice for all is the collective mission. This is at the heart of history for justice. As Becker (1932) reminded us some time ago, history is "more than the memory of things said and done" (p. 225); rather, "it is impossible to divorce history from life . . . [or what the everyperson] needs or desires to do" (p. 227). It is clearer now more than ever that humans need to use history as their guide in building fairer societies at the local, national, and global levels. To do this, we must reorient the purpose of studying the past to better help us reimagine the future. We must use it to ground how we save democracy and set out to make the world better.

We acknowledge that changing the way history has traditionally been taught is a daunting and difficult task. We do not hide the reality that teachers face numerous barriers in doing this justice-oriented work. Yet we also believe that this work is not only possible but also necessary if history education is to become more relevant and useful to citizens. This is not a question of "if we can do this work"; it is a question of "how can we do this work." In this final chapter, we offer some suggestions for how teachers might overcome the typical barriers to creating a classroom focused on history for justice. We start by identifying common pitfalls and, based on research, offer possible ways that those pitfalls might be avoided. We also suggest ways, when pitfalls are unavoidable, that teachers may proactively address the problems that are likely to arise.

OVERCOMING THE BARRIERS TO HISTORY FOR JUSTICE

This section focuses on the four common barriers to enacting history for justice in the classroom: *teacher barriers, student barriers, school and district barriers*, and *community barriers*. We will discuss the barriers and offer ways that teachers might overcome them. Of course, barriers vary from context to context. Some barriers are stronger in certain communities and weaker or nonexistent in others. We do not intend for this section to offer universal solutions; instead, we hope this presents some possible guidance based on the successful justice-oriented teachers we have studied throughout the years. We also hope it helps teachers starting this work to anticipate potential challenges they might face, so they can be the most prepared to negate and react to those challenges.

Teacher Barriers

Many teachers may want to do this work but are or feel underprepared. They may worry that their multicultural historical content knowledge is weak, and they will have difficulty fielding students' questions about nondominant groups (Branch, 2004; Brown & Brown, 2010). They may have experienced history education programs that primarily focused on the histories of dominant groups or the perspectives of those in power, and that is all that they know (Crowley & Smith, 2015; Engebretson, 2018; Hilburn, 2018; King & Chandler, 2016; Marshall et al., 2016; Mayo, 2018; Woodson & Duncan, 2018). They may not know where to start in finding sources or other materials written from people of color, women, LGBTQ people, poor and working classes, or immigrants (Chandler & Hawley, 2017; Crocco, 1997; Engebretson, 2018; Hilburn, 2018; King, 2014; King & Chandler, 2016; Mayo, 2018; Woyshner, 2002). It is difficult to teach what you do not know.

Teachers may also fear that teaching for justice will expose their own prejudiced, discriminatory, or oppressive thinking. As Tatum (1997) has argued,

> Cultural racism—the cultural images and messages that affirm the assumed superiority of Whites and the assumed inferiority of people of color—is like smog in the air. . . . None of us would introduce ourselves as "smog-breathers" . . . but if we live in a smoggy place, how can we avoid breathing the air. . . . [W]e are bombarded with stereotypical images . . . and are rarely informed of the accomplishments of oppressed groups, [so] we will develop the negative categorizations of those groups that form the basis of prejudice. (p. 6)

This concept applies to other forms of discrimination and oppression, whether it is sexism, classism, homophobia, or xenophobia. We live in a society of oppression, and it informs how we view the world.

Teachers who have not examined their own perspectives and biases may worry about making racial blunders (Woodson & Duncan, 2018) or gender- and sexual orientation–related mistakes. As a result, they may choose to avoid race, gender, class, and sexual orientation altogether in their classrooms (Engebretson, 2018; Mayo, 2018; Woodson & Duncan, 2018). Instead, teachers must be constantly learning from their mistakes and finding ways to improve their practice so that it supports all students in their history learning. This work will and should make teachers from dominant groups feel uncomfortable, as it may be a sign of their changing thinking (Woodson & Duncan, 2018). Teachers from dominant groups must become comfortable with the uncomfortable, because it is essential in facing the inequity that has benefited them, and it is a continual part of the process toward being a justice-oriented teacher.

We must, however, also recognize that, in the misguided attempt to teach history for justice, some teachers may commit curricular violence (Brown & Brown, 2010; Gilbert, 2017; Leonardo & Porter, 2010; Shear, 2017). Unlike blunders related to social identity, these acts are never acceptable. For example, monthly or even weekly, we read news stories of teachers using simulations of slavery or racial segregation and asking students to journal as if they were slave owners or White supremacists, as well as White teachers performing imitations of historical people of color (sometimes done in blackface, brownface, yellowface, or redface). While many of these incidents are perpetrated intentionally out of hate or animosity, some of the teachers believed they were instead teaching against discrimination or racism. While incredibly troubling, we do not deny that some of these teachers had thought they were teaching against racism. They may have been so blinded by their racial privilege as White people that they could not see what they were doing was wrong, damaging, or hurtful. However, these teachers are advancing oppression while framing it as benevolence. They are doing the work of supremacy, perhaps without even knowing it. As such, it is essential that we continue to publicize when these actions occur in history classrooms, so they may not continue to happen in the future.

Despite the potential barriers, we argue that teaching history for justice is something that most teachers can and must enact in their classrooms. To overcome these barriers, teachers need preservice and inservice opportunities and continual support for self-reflection, practice, and access to resources. It is crucial that teachers, especially teachers from dominant groups, have guided opportunities to reflect on their own backgrounds and how those backgrounds relate to students' backgrounds (Howard, 2003; Milner, 2003b; Sleeter, 2008). As Milner (2003b) described,

> There is often a void in teachers' reflective thinking where diversity is concerned. For the most part, P-12 classroom teachers have been taught to generally deliberate upon their practices in order to affect change—reflective thinking

that allows them to think about what they are doing and why they are doing it to strengthen and/or transform their practices. But reflection on diversity is seldom taught or practiced. (p. 173)

Instead, reflections on race, gender, class, sexual orientation, and other social identities should be at the core of teacher reflection. Teachers should have regular opportunities to engage in critical dialogue or race-reflective journaling (Milner, 2003a). They should create spaces to share resources (e.g., lesson plans, curricular materials, sources, videos) that are specific to the history classroom (especially if their multicultural content knowledge is limited, which is likely as many university history courses and professional development programs emphasize the histories of dominant groups). This should begin early, during teacher preparation programs, and should continue throughout teachers' careers. This reflective work should be done individually, but also in groups with other educators, who can be critical friends (Nieto, 2000); doing this not only provides important peer support, but also allows for greater group protection (as this work can be difficult or risky in some schools or districts).

We also acknowledge that teachers often have little time for preparation, and if this is a new mode of teaching, it may take substantial time to make adjustments to their practice. This work can more effectively be done with the support of school and district administrators, who intentionally reserve time for teachers to do this work and are willing to provide funds to encourage professional development related to teaching justice. Finally, it is important to acknowledge that this work takes time. Teachers should avoid becoming frustrated if they cannot change their practice overnight. Moreover, they will be able to make changes at different paces.

In Chapter 4, Ms. Becca Luther and Ms. Dana Silva illustrated ways to overcome some of the more difficult teacher barriers. When she set out to center her U.S. history course on the First Nations, through self-reflection, Ms. Luther acknowledged that her Indigenous history content knowledge was limited and that, as a White person, she must do more to challenge her own thinking, which may be guided by settler-colonialism. She developed a critical friendship with Ms. Silva, and they set out to support each other and their colleagues as they rebuilt the curriculum and reinvented their practice. They read numerous books on Indigenous history, attended a professional development program led by local Native educators, and sought new resources and designed new lesson plans that centered authentic Indigenous perspectives. They shared their new pedagogical practices and sought ways to collaborate with other teachers in their department.

Student Barriers

The barriers related to students are different for those from dominant groups compared with those from nondominant groups. For students from dominant groups, it may be incredibly difficult to help them see or acknowledge their social power and privileges. They may have strong beliefs in meritocracy and may be unable to acknowledge that the system is not fair and that some groups benefit from the historical oppression of others. They might suffer from the same "smog" of oppression that teachers from dominant groups might suffer from. On the other hand, for students from nondominant groups, teachers must be careful to not tokenize or essentialize their experiences or histories. They must help elevate these students' ideas and perspectives in the classroom, without putting them on the spot to be the representatives for their identities. Teachers must also acknowledge that conversations about race, gender, class, or sexual orientation can be risky and unsafe for students from nondominant or oppressed groups (Leonardo & Porter, 2010; Woodson & Duncan, 2018), especially if teachers do not approach them with an important level of thoughtfulness and care.

Despite the potential barriers, we argue that teaching history for justice is something that students must experience in their classrooms. To overcome these barriers, teachers need to engage in self-reflection while planning, where they constantly question their own biases and perspectives, as well as question their commitment to seeking diverse and complex voices from underrepresented groups in their history curriculum. For every lesson or assignment, teachers should be asking, "Are there missing people here, and how might they be included in authentic ways?" They need to especially listen to and learn from their students, especially those from nondominant groups, and build bridges to their families. They need to continually develop what Ladson-Billings (2014) called their cultural competence, or "the ability to help students appreciate and celebrate their cultures of origin while gaining knowledge of and fluency in at least one other culture" (p. 75). This should be one of the main goals of any history teacher.

In Chapters 6, 7, and 8, Ms. María Lopez, Mr. Tom Kulig, and Ms. Joyce Smith offered ways to overcome some of the more difficult student barriers. For example, at a predominantly Black and Latinx school, Ms. Lopez built her U.S. history curriculum around the identities of her students (cultural mirrors). In doing so, she centered the narratives of her students and their ancestors in the study of the past. Yet she also understood the importance of helping the students learn about other people's histories and how those histories related to their own family's historical experiences (cultural windows). At a predominantly White school, Mr. Kulig used his classroom to help White students understand how historical oppression led to their current-day social privileges. However, this did not come without controversy. In White spaces, it is not uncommon for Whiteness to obscure reality. Mr. Kulig needed to confront this issue when students or parents pushed back against the idea of critically examining the past (as was the case when a parent demanded that his son not learn about Islam). Mr. Kulig had to routinely practice the delicate balancing act between acknowledging differences in worldviews and sticking to his pedagogical principles. In a predominantly Christian space, Ms. Smith's students pushed back on the idea that other religions had valid beliefs. Instead of discounting her students' religious views, she used their strong faith backgrounds to help them gain a better awareness of their Christian-centric beliefs. While it did not change most students' beliefs, it helped them understand people different than themselves and realize that it is important to stand up for the religious rights and freedoms of all people.

School and District Barriers

The third barrier is found at the school and district level. We speculate that this is where the most resistance to history for justice lies. Included in this resistance are administrators who do not support centering justice in the classroom or are worried it will take time away from district- or state-mandated curricula and assessments (especially when assessments are high stakes). To ensure history for justice is done well, school districts and the leaders in these districts must commit to this mission. They must recruit and hire justice-oriented faculty, with a focus on hiring people of color and people from other unrepresented groups, and create leadership positions centered on providing equity. School and district leaders should encourage their staff to challenge the status quo within schools and use social inquiry to challenge their own practices and policies within the school. They can do this by evaluating the power structures and relationships in their schools around class, race, gender, sexual orientation, language, and other potentially marginalizing categories. Leaders need to provide as many opportunities as possible to receive feedback, specifically from faculty and students of color and from other unrepresented groups, to counteract the traditional assimilationist approaches to the culture and structure of schools. This also involves challenging experienced faculty members to examine their own biases and creating a healthy space for reflective practice. School leaders must encourage students to be activists who fight against oppression at the school, community, and national levels, even if it means protesting and speaking out against policies within their own school. They should create time for social studies and create justice-oriented curriculums.

To be honest, this type of administration does not exist in many schools. Moreover, it is extremely difficult for teachers to do this work if their administration is antithetical or overly concerned about state and federal mandates or standardized tests. Administrators may tell teachers "this work is great but do it on your own time." Or, in some more dire cases, the administrators may believe justice-oriented teaching is wrong or overly political. These factors can make it difficult, or professionally dangerous, to accomplish this work. As such, in some places this work must be done incognito. Teachers must carefully work under the radar of administrators, which also requires a willingness to take professional risks for the betterment of their students.

Teachers must also be able to show how they are addressing state standards *while* ensuring that content and skills found in their curriculum are focused on justice. We know that a mandated history curriculum often presents mainly the perspectives of White, native-born, straight people and men; worse, the curriculum may have embedded anti-Indigenous, racist, sexist, xenophobic, and homophobic ideas (An, 2016; Epstein, 1998; King, 2017; Shear et al., 2015). Often, the mandated history curriculum lists names, dates, and places, but not how those topics should be covered. It rarely prohibits certain historical events, people, or groups from being taught. Justice-oriented history teachers must use the blank spaces of their mandated curriculum as license to remake who is included in the study of the past (and how they are included).

Despite the potential barriers, we argue that teaching history for justice is something that improves a school community. In Chapters 5 and 9, Ana Sanchez and Frank Hashimoto offered examples of ways to overcome some of the more difficult school and district barriers. When Ms. Sanchez's students planned their Black Lives Matter walkout, she was worried the administration would not support this action. To overcome this, she decided to have the students prepare a presentation for the principal. She also prepared her students for the possibility that the administration would say no, and she encouraged them to brainstorm alternative plans. The students discussed reaching out to their community and having the protests out of school during nonschool hours. By having her students present to the principal, she was creating a space for students to work with their administration. However, she also prepared her students to work around the administration by having the students develop alternative plans.

Mr. Hashimoto also had to work around difficult administrative barriers. Many teachers, especially at the elementary level, face the obstacle of not having dedicated time for history in their classrooms. Mr. Hashimoto worked with his principal directly to establish two or three periods a week for social studies, and he also convinced his administration to create a year-end social studies project. In addition to working with his administration to create more time for social studies, he also led his school's equity team, which helped create a supportive environment where this work can flourish. The team runs and recruits professional development for justice-oriented teaching, provides support for colleagues who want to do this work, and hosts collaborative meetings with the staff and the administration about these issues. Overcoming these barriers means a teacher must find ways to increase collaboration with their administration.

Community Barriers

Finally, schools and the teachers who want to make a commitment to justice-oriented teaching must take every opportunity to involve their communities in this work. This involves meeting regularly with parents and guardians, going into the community for home visits, creating forums and spaces to listen to student affinity groups, and attending community events and staying politically active. It is easier to do this work if people in the community see you as "one of them" and know that your intention is to make the community and society better. This work faces less resistance if the parents and community know that your goal is not indoctrination, but that students are being asked to critically examine their world and reach their own conclusions (and that involves interacting with views and perspectives different than their own). Despite the dominant political views of a community (whether they are liberal, conservative, progressive, or libertarian), teachers can face resistance from parents or colleagues in addressing topics of inequity. This can be especially difficult to counteract when there are embedded ethnocentric beliefs about their community's or social group's superiority.

Despite the potential barriers, we argue that teaching history for justice can improve a school community. In Chapters 7 and 9, Mr. Kulig and Mr. Hashimoto offer examples of ways to overcome some of the more difficult community barriers. Prior to the school year, Mr. Hashimoto has in-person meetings with each parent, and he takes time to learn his incoming class's home cultures and languages. Getting to know the families of his students prior to the beginning of the year initiates the process of the community–classroom connection. He is then able to create curricula that represent his students' backgrounds and create outreach projects that address some of the needs in the community.

Several of the imagined teachers in this book also involved the community by inviting local guest speakers to their classrooms, such as Mr. Kulig, who had a local Ghanaian American photographer speak to his students. In addition to bringing in speakers, Mr. Kulig was patient and understanding toward parents who were uncomfortable with the curriculum. When a parent challenged a project about Islam, Mr. Kulig did not change his project. Instead, he met with the parent hoping they could establish trust and come to a shared understanding.

Finally, teachers can work to change preexisting belief structures or policies that perpetuate inequity. Ms. Luther and Ms. Silva had a listening session with the Black Student Union and presented to the school board about changing the name of Columbus Day to Indigenous Peoples' Day. The teachers were finding opportunities to engage with the community, but they also challenged preexisting belief structures. They established trust by reaching out to parents and community members and bringing them into their classrooms as speakers. In general, once those relationships are formed, teachers can work to challenge the status quo or oppressive policies that are often being protected by those with power in the community.

CONCLUSION

The study of history has been relatively unchanged for centuries; when change does occur, it happens very slowly (Barton & Levstik, 2004; Cuban, 2016; Epstein, 2009; VanSledright, 2011; Wineburg, 2001). However, in the past two decades, there have been signs that history education is changing. There have been important shifts in curriculum, teacher preparation, and professional development toward inquiry and more diverse and inclusive representations (Barton & Avery, 2016; Levy et al., 2013). Of course, that does not guarantee that classrooms will change in light of teachers reflecting on these captivating ideas. However, we are hopeful. Most of the teachers we have worked with over the years have wanted to improve their practice and have generally had a broader commitment to justice. Yet they have little support or even time to focus on improving their practice in justice-oriented ways. They have not been afforded opportunities to think deeply about what history for justice would look like or to consider the ways that it could be implemented in their classrooms. We hope this book has offered a thinking piece to help teachers begin envisioning a history classroom that fosters justice-oriented thinking and helps us reimagine a more equitable and fairer world.

References

Accomazzo, S., Moore, M., & Sirojudin, S. (2013). Social justice and religion. In M. J. Austin (Ed.), *Social justice and social work* (pp. 65–82). Sage.

Adichie, C. N. (2009). *The danger of a single story*. TED Conferences.

Al Jazeera English. (2016). *The Crusades: An Arab perspective* [Film]. Author.

An, S. (2016). Asian Americans in American history: An AsianCrit perspective on Asian American inclusion in state U.S. history curriculum standards. *Theory & Research in Social Education, 44*(2), 244–276.

An, S. (2020). Learning racial literacy while navigating White social studies. *The Social Studies, 111*(4), 1–8.

Ananthaswamy, A., & Douglas, K. (2018, April 18). The origins of sexism: How men came to rule 12,000 years ago. *New Scientist.* https://www.newscientist.com/article/mg23831740-400-the-origins-of-sexism-how-men-came-to-rule-12000-years-ago/

Ansary, T. (2009). *Destiny disrupted: A history of the world through Islamic eyes.* PublicAffairs.

Au, W. (2009). Social studies, social justice: W(h)ither the social studies in high-stakes testing? *Teacher Education Quarterly, 36*(1), 43–58.

Ayers, W., Quinn, T., & Stovall, D. (2009). *Handbook of social justice education.* Routledge.

Bagget, H. C., & Simmons, C. G. (2017). A case study of White teacher candidates' conceptions of racial profiling in educational contexts. *Journal of Education, 197*(1), 41–51.

Bailey, G., Shaw, E. L., & Hollifield, D. (2006). The devaluation of social studies in the elementary grades. *Journal of Social Studies Research, 30*(2), 18–29.

Banks, J. A. (2002). Teaching for diversity and unity in a democratic multicultural society. In W. C. Parker (Ed.), *Education for democracy: Contexts, curricula, assessments* (pp. 131–150). Information Age.

Banks, J. A. (2004). Teaching for social justice, diversity, and citizenship in a global world. *Educational Forum, 68*(4), 296–305.

Banks, J. A. (2008). Diversity, group identity, and citizenship education in a global age. *Educational Researcher, 37*(3), 129–139.

Banks, J. A. (2015). Failed citizenship, civic engagement, and education. *Kappa Delta Pi Record, 51*(4), 151–154.

Banks, J. A. (2017). Failed citizenship and transformative civic education. *Educational Researcher, 46*(7), 366–377.

Baron, C. (2012). Understanding historical thinking at historic sites. *Journal of Educational Psychology, 104*(3), 833–847.

Baron, C. (2013). Using inquiry-based instruction to encourage teachers' historical thinking at historic sites. *Teaching and Teacher Education, 35*, 157–169.

Barron, B., & Darling-Hammond, L. (2008). *Teaching for meaningful learning: A review of research on inquiry-based and cooperative learning.* George Lucas Educational Foundation.

Bartholomew, R. E., & Reumschuessel, A. (2018). *American intolerance: Our dark history of demonizing immigrants.* Prometheus.

Barton, K. C. (2002). Review: Historical thinking and other unnatural acts: Charting the future of teaching the past. *Anthropology and Education Quarterly, 33*(4), 272–274.

Barton, K. C., & Avery, P. G. (2016). Research on social studies education: Diverse students, settings, and methods. In D. H. Gitomer & C. A. Bell (Eds.), *Handbook of research on teaching* (5th ed., pp. 985–1038). American Educational Research Association.

Barton, K. C., & Levstik, L. S. (1996). "Back when God was around and everything": Elementary children's understanding of historical time. *American Educational Research Journal, 33*(2), 419–454.

Barton, K. C., & Levstik, L. S. (2003). Why don't more history teachers engage students in interpretation? *Social Education, 67*(6), 358–362.

Barton, K. C., & Levstik, L. S. (2004). *Teaching history for the common good.* Lawrence Erlbaum Associates.

Beck, R. B., Black, L., Krieger, L. S., Naylor, P. C., & Shabaka, D. I. (1999). *World history: Patterns of interaction.* McDougal Littell.

Becker, C. (1932). Everyman his own historian. *American Historical Review, 37*(2), 221–236.

Bishop, R. S. (1990). Mirrors, windows, and sliding glass doors. *Perspectives, 6*(3), ix–xi.

Bolgatz, J. (2005). Revolutionary talk: Elementary teacher and students discuss race in a social studies class. *The Social Studies, 96*(6), 259–264.

Branch, A. J. (2004). Modeling respect by teaching about race and ethnic identity in the social studies. *Theory & Research in Social Education, 32*(4), 523–545.

Bronski, M. (2019). *A queer history of the United States for young people.* Beacon Press.

Brown, K. D., & Brown, A. L. (2010). Silenced memories: An examination of the sociocultural knowledge on race and racial violence in official school curriculum. *Equity & Excellence in Education, 43*(2), 139–154.

Brown, K. D., & Brown, A. L. (2011). Teaching K-8 students about race: African Americans, racism, and the struggle for social justice in the U.S. *Multicultural Education, 19*(1), 9–13.

Brown, M., & Gutiérrez, R. (Illustrator). (2017). *Pelé, king of soccer/El rey del fútbol.* HarperCollins.

Bruchac, J., & Nelson, S. D. (Illustrator). (2008). *Jim Thorpe's bright path.* Lee & Low Books.

Brugar, K., Halvorsen, A.-L., & Hernandez, S. (2014). Where are the women? A classroom inquiry into social studies textbooks. *Social Studies and the Young Learner, 26*(3), 28–31.

Bruner, J. (1960). *The process of education.* Harvard University Press.

Bruner, J. (1970). *Man, a course of study!* Allyn & Bacon.

Busey, C. L. (2014). Examining race from within: Black intraracial discrimination in social studies curriculum. *Social Studies Research and Practice*, 9(2), 120–131.

Busey, C. L., & Cruz, B. C. (2015). A shared heritage: Afro-Latin@s and Black history. *The Social Studies*, 106(6), 293–300.

Busey, C. L., & Walker, I. (2017). A dream and a bus: Black critical patriotism in elementary social studies standards. *Theory & Research in Social Education*, 45(4), 456–488.

Carlone, H. B., Scott, C. M., & Lowder, C. (2014). Becoming (less) scientific: A longitudinal study of students' identity work from elementary to middle school science. *Journal of Research in Science Teaching*, 51(7), 836–869.

Castro, A. J. (2014). The role of teacher education in preparing teachers for critical multicultural citizenship. *Journal of Social Studies Research*, 38, 189–203.

Catholic Church. (1994). *Catechism of the Catholic Church*. Paulist Press.

CBS News. (2013). *CBS News poll, August 7–11, 2013*. https://www.cbsnews.com/news/poll-few-think-all-of-martin-luther-kings-goals-have-been-met/

Chandler, P. T. (2015). What does it mean to "do race" in social studies? In P. T. Chandler (Ed.), *Doing race in social studies: Critical perspectives* (pp. 1–10). Information Age.

Chandler, P. T., & Branscombe, A. (2015). White social studies. In P. T. Chandler (Ed.), *Doing race in social studies: Critical perspectives* (pp. 61–87). Information Age.

Chandler, P. T., & Hawley, T. S. (2017). Using racial-pedagogical-content knowledge and inquiry pedagogy to re-imagine social studies teaching and learning. In P. T. Chandler & T. S. Hawley (Eds.), *Race lessons: Using inquiry to teach about race in social studies* (pp. 1–18). Information Age.

Chandler, P. T., & McKnight, D. (2009). The failure of social education in the United States: A critique of teaching the national story from "White" colourblind eyes. *Journal for Critical Education Policy Studies*, 7(2), 217–248.

Choi, Y. (2013). Teaching social studies for newcomer English language learners: Toward culturally relevant pedagogy. *Multicultural Perspectives*, 15(1), 12–18.

Chumley, C. K. (2013, September 6). Rush Limbaugh's new book: "True story on Thanksgiving . . . no politics in this." *Washington Times*. https://www.washingtontimes.com/news/2013/sep/6/rush-limbaughs-new-book-true-story-thanksgiving-no/

Clauss, K. S. (2017, March 3). Bill introduced to ban Howard Zinn books from public schools. *Boston Magazine*. https://www.bostonmagazine.com/news/2017/03/03/howard-zinn-books-ban-bill/

Colburn, A. (2000). An inquiry primer. *Science Scope*, 23(6), 42–44.

Conrad, J. (2019). The Big History Project and colonizing knowledges in world history curriculum. *Journal of Curriculum Studies*, 51(1), 1–20.

Coogler, R. (Director). (2018). *Black panther* [Film]. Walt Disney Studios.

Cooks, B. R. (2007). Fixing race: Visual representations of African Americans at the World's Columbian Exposition, Chicago, 1893. *Patterns of Prejudice*, 41(5), 435–465.

Cox, D., & Jones, R. P. (2016). *Two-thirds of Trump supporters say nation needs a leader willing to break the rules*. PRRI/The Atlantic.

Crenshaw, K. (1991). Mapping the margins: Intersectionality, identity politics, and violence against women of color. *Stanford Law Review*, 43(6), 1241–1299.

Crocco, M. S. (1997). Making time for women's history. *Social Education, 61*(1), 32–37.

Crocco, M. S. (2001). The missing discourse about gender and sexuality in the social studies. *Theory into Practice, 40*(1), 65–71.

Crocco, M. S. (2010). Teaching about women in world history. *The Social Studies, 102*(1), 18–24.

Crowley, R. M., & Smith, W. (2015). Whiteness and social studies teacher education: Tensions in the pedagogical task. *Teaching Education, 26*(2), 160–178.

Cuban, L. (2016). *Teaching history then and now: A story of stability and change in schools.* Harvard Education Press.

Cvencek, D., Meltzoff, A. N., & Greenwald, A. G. (2011). Math–gender stereotypes in elementary school children. *Child Development, 82*(3), 766–779.

Dahlum, S., Knutsen, C. H., & Wig, T. (2019). Who revolts? Empirically revisiting the social origins of democracy. *Journal of Politics, 81*(4), 1494–1499.

Davis, A. Y. (1981). *Women, race & class.* Vintage.

Davis, A. Y. (2011). *Abolition democracy: Beyond empire, prisons, and torture.* Seven Stories Press.

Davis, A. Y. (2016). *Freedom is a constant struggle: Ferguson, Palestine, and the foundations of a movement.* Haymarket Books.

Delacampagne, C. (1983). *L'Invention du racisme: Antiquité et Moyen Age.* Fayard.

Delgado, R., & Stefancic, J. (2012). *Critical race theory: An introduction.* New York University Press.

Dewey, J. (1997). *How we think.* Dover. (Original work published 1910)

Dillard, C., Duncan, K. E., & Johnson, L. (2017). Black history full circle: Lessons from a Ghana study abroad in education program. *Social Education, 81*(1), 50–53.

Donaldson, M. (1979). *Children's minds.* W. W. Norton & Company.

Dozono, T. (in press). The passive voice of White supremacy: Tracing epistemic and discursive violence in world history curriculum. *Review of Education, Pedagogy, and Cultural Studies.*

Drutman, L., Diamond, L., & Goldman, J. (2018). *Follow the leader: Exploring American support for democracy and authoritarianism.* Democracy Fund Voter Study Group.

DuBois, D. L., Burk-Braxton, C., Swenson, L. P., Tevendale, H. D., & Hardesty, J. L. (2002). Race and gender influences on adjustment in early adolescence: Investigation of an integrative model. *Child Development, 73*(5), 1573–1592.

Dunbar-Ortiz, R. (2015). *An Indigenous peoples' history of the United States.* Beacon Press.

Duncan, K. E. (2019). "They hate on me!" Black teachers interrupting their White colleagues' racism. *Educational Studies, 55*(2), 197–213.

Dunn, A. (2018). *Partisans are divided over the fairness of the U.S. economy—and why people are rich or poor.* Pew Research Center.

Dunn, R. E. (2008). The two world histories. *Social Education, 72*(5), 257–263.

Dyble, M., Salali, G. D., Chaudhary, N., Page, A., Smith, D., Thompson, J., Vinicius, R., Mace, A. B., & Migliano, A. (2015). Sex equality can explain the unique social structure of hunter-gatherer bands. *Science, 348*(6236), 796–798.

Elechi, O. O. (2004). *Human rights and the African indigenous justice system.* Paper presented at the 18th International Conference of the International Society for the Reform of Criminal Law, Montréal, Canada.

Ellington, L., Leming, J. S., & Schug, M. (2006). The state of social studies: A national random survey of elementary and middle school social studies teachers. *Social Education, 70*(5), 322–324.

Ellis, E. G., & Esler, A. (2005). *World history: Connections to today.* Pearson Prentice Hall.

Emdin, C. (2011). Moving beyond the boat without a paddle: Reality pedagogy, Black youth, and urban science education. *Journal of Negro Education, 80*(3), 284–295.

Endacott, J. L. (2005). It's not all ancient history now: Connecting the past by weaving a threaded historical concept. *The Social Studies, 96*(5), 227–231.

Engebretson, K. E. (2018). Toward a gender inclusive vision for powerful and authentic social studies. In C. C. Martell (Ed.), *Social studies teacher education: Critical issues and current perspectives* (pp. 113–132). Information Age.

Epstein, T. (1998). Deconstructing differences in African-American and European-American adolescents' perspectives on U.S. history. *Curriculum Inquiry, 28*(4), 397–423.

Epstein, T. (2009). *Interpreting national history: Race, identity, and pedagogy in classrooms and communities.* Routledge.

Epstein, T., & Gist, C. (2015). Teaching racial literacy in secondary humanities classrooms: Challenging adolescents' of color concepts of race and racism. *Race, Ethnicity and Education, 18*(1), 40–60.

Epstein, T., Mayorga, E., & Nelson, J. (2011). Teaching about race in an urban history class: The effects of culturally responsive teaching. *Journal of Social Studies Research, 35*(1), 2–21.

Evans, R. W., Avery, P. G., & Pederson, P. V. (1999). Taboo topics: Cultural restraint on teaching social issues. *The Social Studies, 90*(5), 218–224.

Femincide Watch. (2019). *Study on global homicide: Gender-related killings of women and girls.* Author.

Fitchett, P. G., & Heafner, T. L. (2010). A national perspective on the effects of high-stakes testing and standardization on elementary social studies marginalization. *Theory & Research in Social Education, 38*(1), 114–130.

Fitchett, P. G., Heafner, T. L., & Lambert, R. G. (2014a). Assessment, autonomy, and elementary social studies time. *Teachers College Record, 116*(10), 1–34.

Fitchett, P. G., Heafner, T. L., & Lambert, R. G. (2014b). Examining elementary social studies marginalization: A multilevel model. *Educational Policy, 28*(1), 40–68.

Fitchett, P. G., Heafner, T. L., & VanFossen, P. J. (2014). An analysis of time prioritization for social studies in elementary school classrooms. *Journal of Curriculum and Instruction, 8*(2), 7–35.

Foa, R. S., & Mounk, Y. (2016). The democratic disconnect. *Journal of Democracy, 27*(3), 5–17.

Foner, E. (2017). *A short history of reconstruction.* Harper Collins. (Original work published 1990)

Fonte, J. D. (1994). Standards for world history: What do students most need to know? *Journal of Education, 176*(3), 73–81.

Frankopan, P. (2015). *The silk roads: A new history of the world.* Vintage.

Freire, P. (1974). *Pedagogy of the oppressed.* Seabury.

Freire, P. (2000). *Pedagogy of the oppressed* (M. B. Ramos, Trans.). Continuum. (Original work published 1970)

Freire, P., & Macedo, D. (2005). *Literacy: Reading the word and the world*. Routledge.

Friedersdorf, C. (2014, August 6). Using Rush Limbaugh to teach the Civil War to 3rd graders. *The Atlantic*. https://www.theatlantic.com/politics/archive/2014/08/3rd-grade-teacher-uses-rush-limbaugh-book-to-teach-the-civil-war/375633/

Gagnon, P. (1989). *Historical literacy: The case for history in American education*. Houghton Mifflin.

Gagnon, P. (1998). Teaching the West and the world from the Massachusetts framework. *Journal of Education, 180*(1), 67–78.

Galeano, E. (1997). *Open veins of Latin America: Five centuries of the pillage of a continent*. New York University Press.

Gilbert, L. (2017). Notes on understanding and valuing the anger of students marginalized by the social studies curriculum. In P. T. Chandler & T. S. Hawley (Eds.), *Race lessons: Using inquiry to teach about race in social studies* (pp. 379–395). Information Age.

Girard, B., & Harris, L. M. (2013). Considering world history as a space for developing global citizenship competencies. *Educational Forum, 77*(4), 438–449.

Golenbock, P., & Bacon, P. (Illustrator). (1992). *Teammates*. HMH Books for Young Readers.

Grant, S. G., Swan, K., & Lee, J. (2017). *Inquiry-based practice in social studies education: Understanding the inquiry design model*. Routledge.

Green, E. (2015, December 16). The fear of Islam in Tennessee public schools. *The Atlantic*. https://www.theatlantic.com/education/archive/2015/12/fear-islam-tennessee-public-schools/420441/

Gutiérrez, G. (1988). *A theology of liberation: History, politics, and salvation*. Orbis Books.

Hahn, C. L., Bernard-Powers, J., Crocco, M. S., & Woyshner, C. (2007). Gender equity in social studies. In S. Klein, B. Richardson, & D. A. Grayson (Eds.), *Handbook for achieving gender equity through education* (pp. 335–358). Routledge.

Hannah-Jones, N. (2019). The 1619 project. *The New York Times Magazine*. https://www.nytimes.com/interactive/2019/08/14/magazine/1619-america-slavery.html

Harris, L. M. (2014). Making connections for themselves and their students: Examining teachers' organization of world history. *Theory & Research in Social Education, 42*(3), 336–374.

Harris, L. M., & Girard, B. (2014). Instructional significance for teaching history: A preliminary framework. *Journal of Social Studies Research, 38*(4), 215–225.

Harvard Opinion Research Program. (2018). *Discrimination in America*. Robert Wood Johnson Foundation and National Public Radio.

Hassan, A. (2019, November 12). Hate-crime violence hits 16-year high, F.B.I. reports. *The New York Times*. https://www.nytimes.com/2019/11/12/us/hate-crimes-fbi-report.html

Hawkins, S., Yudkin, D., Juan-Torres, M., & Dixon, T. (2018). *Hidden tribes: A study of America's polarized landscape* (Vol. 5). More in Common.

Hawkman, A. M. (2018). Exposing whiteness in the elementary social studies methods classroom: In pursuit of developing antiracist teacher education candidates. In S. B. Shear, C. M. Tschida, E. Bellows, L. B. Buchanan, & E. E. Saylor (Eds.), *(Re)imagining elementary social studies: A controversial reader* (pp. 49–71). Information Age.

Hawkman, A. M., & Castro, A. J. (2017). The long civil rights movement: Expanding Black history in the social studies classroom. *Social Education*, *81*(1), 28–32.

Heafner, T. L., & Fitchett, P. G. (2012a). National trends in elementary instruction: Exploring the role of social studies curricula. *The Social Studies*, *103*(2), 67–72.

Heafner, T. L., & Fitchett, P. G. (2012b). Tipping the scales: National trends of declining social studies instructional time in elementary schools. *Journal of Social Studies Research*, *36*(2), 190–215.

Helms, J. E. (1990). *Black and White racial identity: Theory, research, and practice.* Greenwood.

Helms, J. E. (1995). An update of Helm's White and people of color racial identity models. In J. G. Ponterotto, J. M. Casas, L. A. Suzuki, & C. M. Alexander (Eds.), *Handbook of multicultural counseling* (pp. 181–198). Sage.

Hilburn, J. (2018). Immigration and social studies teacher education. In C. C. Martell (Ed.), *Social studies teacher education: Critical issues and current perspectives* (pp. 151–174). Information Age.

Hill, P. W., McQuillan, J., Spiegel, A. N., & Diamond, J. (2018). Discovery orientation, cognitive schemas, and disparities in science identity in early adolescence. *Sociological Perspectives*, *61*(1), 99–125.

Hilton, A. A. (2017, November 12). Prominent scholar calls growth mindset a "cancerous" idea, in isolation. https://www.huffpost.com/entry/prominent-scholar -calls-growth-mindset-a-cancerous_b_5a07f046e4b0f1dc729a6bc3

Hochschild, A. (1999). *King Leopold's ghost: A story of greed, terror, and heroism in colonial Africa.* Houghton Mifflin Harcourt.

Holcomb-McCoy, C. (2005). Ethnic identity development in early adolescence: Implications and recommendations for middle school counselors. *Professional School Counseling*, *9*(2), 120–127.

Horowitz, J. M., Brown, A., & Cox, K. (2019). *Race in America 2019.* Pew Research Center.

Horowitz, J. M., Parker, K., & Stepler, R. (2017). *Wide partisan gaps in U.S. over how far the country has come on gender equality.* Pew Research Center.

Hourdakis, A. (1996). A global dimension via the teaching of the "ancient world": Theoretical concepts and an empirical approach from Greek primary textbooks. *Mediterranean Journal of Educational Studies*, *1*(2), 157–182.

Hourdakis, A., Calogiannakis, P., & Chiang, T.-H. (2018). Teaching history in a global age. *History Education Research Journal*, *15*(2), 328–341.

Howard, T. C. (2003). Culturally relevant pedagogy: Ingredients for critical teacher reflection. *Theory into Practice*, *42*(3), 195–202.

Howard, T. C., & del Rosario, C. D. (2000). Talking race in teacher education: The need for racial dialogue in teacher education programs. *Action in Teacher Education*, *21*(4), 127–137.

Human Rights Campaign Foundation. (2019). *A national epidemic: Fatal anti-transgender violence in America in 2019.* Author.

Husband, T. (2010). He's too young to learn about that stuff: Anti-racist pedagogy and early childhood social studies. *Social Studies Research and Practice*, *5*(2), 61–75.

Ipsos. (2019). *January 11–15, 2019, Ipsos poll.* https://www.ipsos.com/en-us/news -polls/90-favorability-rating-martin-luther-king-jr-2019-01-18

Irani, K. D., & Silver, M. (1995). *Social justice in the ancient world*. Greenwood.

Isaac, B. (2004). *The invention of racism in classical antiquity*. Princeton University Press.

Jackson, B. (2005). The conceptual history of social justice. *Political Studies Review*, *3*(3), 356–373.

Jacobson, M. F. (1999). *Whiteness of a different color: European immigrants and the alchemy of race*. Harvard University Press.

James, J. H. (2008). Teachers as protectors: Making sense of preservice teachers' resistance to interpretation in elementary history teaching. *Theory & Research in Social Education*, *36*(3), 172–205.

Johnson, A., & Peck, B. (Illustrator). (2007). *Just like Josh Gibson*. Simon & Schuster Books for Young Readers.

Jones, E. B., Pang, V. O., & Rodríguez, J. L. (2001). Social studies in the elementary classroom: Culture matters. *Theory into Practice*, *40*(1), 35–41.

Jones, M. H., Hackel, T. S., Hershberger, M. A., & Goodrich, K. M. (2019). Queer youth in educational psychology research. *Journal of Homosexuality*, *66*(13), 1797–1816.

Joyce, B., Weil, M., & Calhoun, E. (2004). *Models of teaching* (7th ed.). Pearson.

Kahne, J. E., & Middaugh, E. (2008). High quality civic education: What is it and who gets it? *Social Education*, *72*(1), 34–39.

Kane, J. M. (2012). Young African American children constructing academic and disciplinary identities in an urban science classroom. *Science Education*, *96*(3), 457–487.

Kendi, I. X. (2017). *Stamped from the beginning: The definitive history of racist ideas in America*. Nation Books.

Kendi, I. X. (2019). *How to be an antiracist*. One World.

Kim, M. (2018). Understanding children's science identity through classroom interactions. *International Journal of Science Education*, *40*(1), 24–45.

King, L. J. (2014). Learning other people's history: Pre-service teachers' developing African American historical knowledge. *Teaching Education*, *25*(4), 427–456.

King, L. J. (2016). Teaching Black history as a racial literacy project. *Race, Ethnicity and Education*, *19*(6), 1303–1318.

King, L. J. (2017). The status of Black history in U.S. schools and society. *Social Education*, *81*(1), 14–18.

King, L. J., & Brown, K. (2014). Once a year to be Black: Fighting against typical Black History Month pedagogies. *Negro Educational Review*, *65*(1–4), 23–43.

King, L. J., & Chandler, P. T. (2016). From non-racism to anti-racism in social studies teacher education: Social studies and racial pedagogical content knowledge. In A. R. Crowe & A. Cuenca (Eds.), *Rethinking social studies teacher education in the twenty-first century* (pp. 3–21). Springer.

King, L. J., & Womac, P. (2014). A bundle of silences: Examining the racial representation of Black founding fathers of the United States through Glenn Beck's Founders' Fridays. *Theory & Research in Social Education*, *42*(1), 35–64.

King, L. J., & Woodson, A. N. (2017). Baskets of cotton and birthday cakes: Teaching slavery in social studies classrooms. *Social Studies Education Review*, *6*(1), 1–18.

King, L. J., Davis, C., & Brown, A. L. (2012). African American history, race, and textbooks: An examination of the works of Harold O. Rugg and Carter G. Woodson. *Journal of Social Studies Research*, *36*(4), 359–386.

King, L. J., Gardner-McCune, C., Vargas, P., & Jimenez, Y. (2014). Re-discovering and re-creating African American historical accounts through mobile apps: The role of mobile technology in history education. *Journal of Social Studies Research*, *38*(3), 173–188.

Klein, M. M. (1985). Everyman his own historian: Carl Becker as historiographer. *The History Teacher*, *19*(1), 101–109.

Kochhar, R., & Cilluffo, A. (2018). *Key findings on the rise in income inequality within America's racial and ethnic groups*. Pew Research Center.

Ladson-Billings, G. (1995a). But that's just good teaching! The case for culturally relevant pedagogy. *Theory into Practice*, *34*(3), 159–165.

Ladson-Billings, G. (1995b). Toward a theory of culturally relevant pedagogy. *American Educational Research Journal*, *32*(3), 465–491.

Ladson-Billings, G. (2003). Lies my teacher still tells: Developing a critical race perspective toward the social studies. In G. Ladson-Billings (Ed.), *Critical race theory perspectives on the social studies: The profession, policies, and curriculum* (pp. 1–11). Information Age.

Ladson-Billings, G. (2006). "Yes, but how do we do it?": Practicing culturally relevant pedagogy. In J. Landsman & C. W. Lewis (Eds.), *White teachers, diverse classrooms: Creating inclusive schools, building on students' diversity, and providing true educational equity* (pp. 29–41). Stylus.

Ladson-Billings, G. (2009). *The dreamkeepers: Successful teachers of African American children* (2nd ed.). Jossey-Bass.

Ladson-Billings, G. (2014). Culturally relevant pedagogy 2.0: aka the remix. *Harvard Educational Review*, *84*(1), 74–84.

Ladson-Billings, G. (2015). *Justice . . . just, justice*. Paper presented at the Annual Meeting of the American Educational Research Association, Chicago, IL.

Ladson-Billings, G., & Tate, W. F. (1995). Toward a critical race theory of education. *Teachers College Record*, *97*(1), 11–30.

Lakey, B., Lakey, G., Napier, R., & Robinson, J. (2016). *Grassroots and nonprofit leadership: A guide for organizations in changing times*. New Society.

Lakey, G. (2004). Strategizing for a living revolution. In D. Solnit (Ed.), *Globalize liberation: How to uproot the system and build a better world* (pp. 135–160). City Lights Books.

LeCompte, K., Blevins, B., & Riggers-Piehl, T. (in press). Developing civic competence through action civics: A longitudinal look at the data. *Journal of Social Studies Research*.

Leonardo, Z., & Porter, R. K. (2010). Pedagogy of fear: Toward a Fanonian theory of "safety" in race dialogue. *Race, Ethnicity and Education*, *13*(2), 139–157.

Lévesque, S. (2008). *Thinking historically: Educating students for the twenty-first century*. University of Toronto Press.

Levitsky, S., & Ziblatt, D. (2018). *How democracies die*. Crown.

Levstik, L. S., & Barton, K. C. (2001). *Doing history: Investigating with children in elementary and middle schools* (2nd ed.). Lawrence Erlbaum Associates.

Levstik, L. S., & Barton, K. C. (2011). *Doing history: Investigating with children in elementary and middle schools* (4th ed.). Routledge.

Levy, B. L. M., Thomas, E. E., Drago, K., & Rex, L. A. (2013). Examining studies of inquiry-based learning in three fields of education: Sparking generative conversation. *Journal of Teacher Education*, *64*(5), 387–408.

Love, B. L. (2019). *We want to do more than survive: Abolitionist teaching and the pursuit of educational freedom.* Beacon Press.

Lowenthal, D. (2000). Dilemmas and delights of learning history. In P. N. Stearns, P. C. Seixas, & S. S. Wineburg (Eds.), *Knowing, teaching, and learning history: National and international perspectives* (pp. 63–82). New York University Press.

Madison, J. (1788). The federalist papers: No. 51. https://avalon.law.yale.edu/18th_century/fed51.asp

Magill, K. R., & Salinas, C. (2019). The primacy of relation: Social studies teachers and the praxis of critical pedagogy. *Theory & Research in Social Education,* 47(1), 1–28.

Manning, M. L. (1993). Cultural and gender differences in young adolescents. *Middle School Journal,* 25(1), 13–17.

Marino, M. (2010). World history and teacher education: Challenges and possibilities. *The Social Studies,* 102(1), 3–8.

Marri, A. R. (2005). Building a framework for classroom-based multicultural democratic education: Learning from three skilled teachers. *Teachers College Record,* 107(5), 1036–1059.

Marshall, P. L., Manfra, M. M., & Simmons, C. G. (2016). No more playing in the dark: Twenty-first century citizenship, critical race theory, and the future of the social studies methods course. In A. R. Crowe & A. Cuenca (Eds.), *Rethinking social studies teacher education in the twenty-first century* (pp. 61–79). Springer.

Martell, C. C. (2013). Learning to teach history as interpretation: A longitudinal study of beginning teachers. *Journal of Social Studies Research,* 37(1), 17–31.

Martell, C. C. (2013). Race and histories: Examining culturally relevant teaching in the U.S. history classroom. *Theory & Research in Social Education,* 41(1), 65–88.

Martell, C. C. (2015). Learning to teach culturally relevant social studies: A White teacher's retrospective self-study. In P. T. Chandler (Ed.), *Doing race in social studies: Critical perspectives* (pp. 41–60). Information Age.

Martell, C. C. (2016). Divergent views of race: Examining Whiteness in the U.S. history classroom. *Social Studies Research and Practice,* 11(1), 93–111.

Martell, C. C. (2017). Approaches to teaching race in elementary social studies: A case study of preservice teachers. *Journal of Social Studies Research,* 41(1), 75–87.

Martell, C. C. (2018). Teaching race in U.S. history: Examining culturally relevant pedagogy in a multicultural urban high school. *Journal of Education,* 198(1), 63–77.

Martell, C. C. (2020). Barriers to inquiry-based instruction: A longitudinal study of history teachers. *Journal of Teacher Education,* 71(3), 279–291.

Martell, C. C., & Stevens, K. M. (2017a). Becoming a race-conscious social studies teacher: The influence of personal and professional experiences. *The Social Studies,* 108(6), 249–260.

Martell, C. C., & Stevens, K. M. (2017b). Equity- and tolerance-oriented teachers: Approaches to teaching race in the social studies classroom. *Theory & Research in Social Education,* 45(4), 489–516.

Martell, C. C., & Stevens, K. M. (2019). Culturally sustaining social studies teachers: Understanding models of practice. *Teaching and Teacher Education,* 86, 1–11.

Martin, D., & Monte-Sano, C. (2008). Inquiry, controversy, and ambiguous texts: Learning to teach for historical thinking. In W. J. Warren & D. A. Cantu (Eds.), *History Education 101: The past, present, and future of teacher preparation* (pp. 167–186). Information Age.

Martinelle, R., Martell, C. C., & Chalmers, J. P. (2019). *Teaching for democracy in multicultural settings: A study of beginning teachers and citizenship education.* Paper presented at the American Educational Research Association, Toronto, Canada.

May, S., & Sleeter, C. E. (Eds.). (2010). *Critical multiculturalism: Theory and praxis.* Routledge.

Mayes, E., Mitra, D. L., & Serriere, S. C. (2016). Figured worlds of citizenship: Examining differences made in "making a difference" in an elementary school classroom. *American Educational Research Journal, 53*(3), 605–638.

Mayo, J. B. (2007). Negotiating sexual orientation and classroom practice(s) at school. *Theory & Research in Social Education, 35*(3), 447–464.

Mayo, J. B. (2018). Where is the queerness in social studies teacher education? In C. C. Martell (Ed.), *Social studies teacher education: Critical issues and current perspectives* (pp. 133–149). Information Age.

Merriam-Webster. (2019). Social. In *Merriam-Webster dictionary.* https://www.merriam-webster.com/dictionary/social?utm_campaign=sd&utm_medium=serp&utm_source=jsonld

Milner, H. R. (2003a). Reflection, racial competence, and critical pedagogy: How do we prepare pre-service teachers to pose tough questions? *Race, Ethnicity and Education, 6*(2), 193–208.

Milner, H. R. (2003b). Teacher reflection and race in cultural contexts: History, meanings, and methods in teaching. *Theory into Practice, 42*(3), 173–180.

Minardi, M. (2010). *Making slavery history: Abolitionism and the politics of memory in Massachusetts.* Oxford University Press.

Mochizuki, K., & Lee, D. (Illustrator). (2009). *Baseball saved us.* Harcourt School Publishers.

Monte-Sano, C. (2008). Qualities of historical writing instruction: A comparative case study of two teachers' practices. *American Educational Research Journal, 45*(4), 1045–1079.

Monte-Sano, C. (2010). Disciplinary literacy in history: An exploration of the historical nature of adolescents' writing. *Journal of the Learning Sciences, 19*(4), 539–568.

Monte-Sano, C. (2016). Argumentation in history classrooms: A key path to understanding the discipline and preparing citizens. *Theory into Practice, 55*(4), 311–319.

Morris, I., & Scheidel, W. (2016). What is ancient history? *Daedalus, 145*(2), 113–121.

Moyer, B., MacAllister, J., Finley, M. L., & Soifer, S. (2001). *Doing democracy: The MAP model for organizing social movements.* New Society Publishers.

Myers, J. P. (2006). Rethinking the social studies curriculum in the context of globalization: Education for global citizenship in the U.S. *Theory & Research in Social Education, 34*(3), 370–394.

Nas. (2003). I can. [Song]. On *God's son.* Ill Will, Columbia Records.

Nash, G. B., Crabtree, C., & Dunn, R. E. (2000). *History on trial: Culture wars and the teaching of the past.* Random House.

Nieto, S. (2000). Placing equity front and center: Some thoughts on transforming teacher education for a new century. *Journal of Teacher Education, 51*(3), 180–187.

Noddings, N. (2001). The care tradition: Beyond "add women and stir." *Theory into Practice, 40*(1), 29–34.

Ogburn, W. F. (1926). The great man versus social forces. *Social Forces, 5*(2), 225–231.

Ohlheiser, A. (2013, July 16). Former governor, now Purdue president, wanted Howard Zinn banned in schools. *The Atlantic.* https://www.theatlantic.com/national/archive/2013/07/former-ind-gov-daniels-now-purdue-president-wanted-howard-zinn-banned-schools/313256/

Oppenheimer, M., & Lakey, G. (1965). *A manual for direct action: Strategy and tactics for civil rights and all other nonviolent protest movements.* Quadrangle Books.

Oto, R. (2020). "This isn't a sentence in a history book": Students of color resistance to official knowledges of Whiteness. In A. M. Hawkman & S. B. Shear (Eds.), *Marking the "invisible": Articulating Whiteness in social studies education* (pp. 217–236). Information Age.

Oto, R., & Chikkatur, A. (in press). "We didn't have to go through those barriers": Culturally affirming learning in a high school affinity group. *Journal of Social Studies Research*, 1–13.

Packer, G. (2018). A new report offers insights into tribalism in the age of Trump. *The New Yorker,* https://www.newyorker.com/news/daily-comment/a-new-report-offers-insights-into-tribalism-in-the-age-of-trump

Paddon, A. R., & Turner, S. (1995). African Americans and the World's Columbian Exposition. *Illinois Historical Journal, 88*(1), 19–36.

Paris, D. (2012). Culturally sustaining pedagogy: A needed change in stance, terminology, and practice. *Educational Researcher, 41*(3), 93–97.

Paris, D., & Alim, H. S. (2014). What are we seeking to sustain through culturally sustaining pedagogy? A loving critique forward. *Harvard Educational Review, 84*(1), 85–100.

Paris, D., & Alim, H. S. (Eds.). (2017). *Culturally sustaining pedagogies: Teaching and learning for justice in a changing world.* Teachers College Press.

Parker, W. C. (2008). *Social studies in elementary education.* Allyn & Bacon.

Piaget, J. (1950/2001). *The psychology of intelligence.* Routledge.

Piaget, J. (1970). *Science of education and the psychology of the child.* Orion Press.

Quintana, S. M. (1998). Children's developmental understanding of ethnicity and race. *Applied and Preventive Psychology, 7*(1), 27–45.

Ramírez, S. E., Stearns, P. N., & Wineburg, S. S. (2008). *Holt World history: Human legacy.* Holt, Rinehart, and Winston.

Ramsey, P. G. (1991). Young children's awareness and understanding of social class differences. *Journal of Genetic Psychology, 152*(1), 71–82.

Ravitch, D. (1990). Multiculturalism: E pluribus plures. *American Scholar, 59*(3), 337–354.

Ravitch, D., & Finn, C. E. (1987). *What do our 17-year-olds know? A report on the first National Assessment of History and Literature.* Harper & Row.

Rawls, J. (1991). Justice as fairness: Political not metaphysical. *Philosophy & Public Affairs, 14*(3), 223–251.

Rawls, J. (1999). *A theory of justice*. Harvard University Press. (Original work published 1971)

Reed, C. R. (2002). *"All the world is here!": The Black presence at White City*. Indiana University Press.

Reisman, A. (2012a). The "document-based lesson": Bringing disciplinary inquiry into high school history classrooms with adolescent struggling readers. *Journal of Curriculum Studies, 44*(2), 233–264.

Reisman, A. (2012b). Reading like a historian: A document-based history curriculum intervention in urban high schools. *Cognition and Instruction, 30*(1), 86–112.

Reisman, A., & Wineburg, S. S. (2008). Teaching the skill of contextualizing in history. *The Social Studies, 99*(5), 202–207.

Richardson, V. (Ed.). (1997). *Constructivist teacher education: Building a world of new understandings*. Falmer Press.

Risinger, C. F. (1995). The National History Standards: A view from the inside. *The History Teacher, 28*(3), 387–393.

Rodríguez, N. N. (2018). From margins to center: Developing cultural citizenship education through the teaching of Asian American history. *Theory & Research in Social Education, 46*(4), 528–573.

Rodríguez, N. N. (in press-a). Focus on friendship or fights for civil rights? Teaching the difficult history of Japanese American incarceration through The Bracelet. *Bank Street Occasional Papers Series*.

Rodríguez, N. N. (in press-b). Much bigger than a hamburger: Disrupting problematic picturebook depictions of the civil rights movement. *International Journal of Multicultural Education*.

Roediger, D. R. (2006). *Working toward Whiteness: How America's immigrants became White: The strange journey from Ellis Island to the suburbs*. Basic Books.

Rudwick, E. M., & Meier, A. (1965). Black man in the "White City": Negroes and the Columbian Exposition, 1893. *Phylon, 26*(4), 354–361.

Salinas, C. S., & Blevins, B. (2014). Critical historical inquiry: How might preservice teachers confront master historical narratives? *Social Studies Research and Practice, 9*(3), 35–50.

Salinas, C. S., Blevins, B., & Sullivan, C. C. (2012). Critical historical thinking: When official narratives collide with other narratives. *Multicultural Perspectives, 14*(1), 18–27.

Santiago, M. (2017). Erasing differences for the sake of inclusion: How Mexican/Mexican American students construct historical narratives. *Theory & Research in Social Education, 45*(1), 43–74.

Santiago, M. (2019). Historical inquiry to challenge the narrative of racial progress. *Cognition and Instruction, 37*(1), 93–117.

Santiago, M., & Castro, E. (in press). Teaching anti-essentialist historical inquiry. *The Social Studies*.

Schonberger, H. (1974). Purposes and ends in history: Presentism and the New Left. *The History Teacher, 7*(3), 448–458.

Seixas, P., & Morton, T. (2013). *The big six: Historical thinking concepts*. Nelson Education.

Semega, J., Kollar, M., Creamer, J., & Mohanty, A. (2019). *Income and poverty in the United States: 2018*. U.S. Census Bureau.

Sen, A. K. (2009). *The idea of justice.* Harvard University Press.

Serriere, S. C. (2019). Social studies in the early years: Children engaging as citizens through the social sciences. In C. P. Brown, M. B. McMullen, & N. File (Eds.), *The Wiley handbook of early childhood care and education* (pp. 377–399). John Wiley & Sons.

Shear, S. B. (2017). Foreword. In P. T. Chandler & T. S. Hawley (Eds.), *Race lessons: Using inquiry to teach about race in social studies* (pp. ix–xii). Information Age.

Shear, S. B., Knowles, R. T., Soden, G. J., & Castro, A. J. (2015). Manifesting destiny: Re/presentations of Indigenous peoples in K–12 U.S. history standards. *Theory & Research in Social Education, 43*(1), 68–101.

Shutts, K. (2015). Young children's preferences: Gender, race, and social status. *Child Development Perspectives, 9*(4), 262–266.

Sleeter, C. E. (2008). Preparing White teachers for diverse students. In M. Cochran-Smith, S. Feiman-Nemser, D. J. McIntyre, & K. E. Demers (Eds.), *Handbook of research in teacher education: Enduring questions in changing contexts* (pp. 559–582). Lawrence Erlbaum Associates.

Solorzano, D. G., & Yosso, T. J. (2002). Critical race methodology: Counter-storytelling as an analytical framework for education research. *Qualitative Inquiry, 8*(1), 23–44.

Stearns, P. N. (1998). Why study history? American Historical Association. https://www.historians.org/pubs/Free/WhyStudyHistory.htm

Stern, S. M. (1994). Beyond the rhetoric: An historian's view of the "national" standards for United States history. *Journal of Education, 176*(3), 61–71.

Stern, S. M. (1998). Improving history education for all students: The Massachusetts History and Social Science Curriculum Framework. *Journal of Education, 180*(1), 1–13.

Stevens, K. M., & Martell, C. C. (2016). An avenue for challenging sexism: Examining the high school sociology classroom. *Journal of Social Science Education, 15*(1), 63–73.

Stevens, K. M., & Martell, C. C. (2019). Feminist social studies teachers: The role of teachers' backgrounds and beliefs in shaping gender-equitable practices. *Journal of Social Studies Research, 43*(1), 1–16.

Stotsky, S. (2004). *The stealth curriculum: Manipulating America's history teachers.* Thomas B. Fordham Foundation.

Sutter, F. (2018). Putting a new face, and new faces, on the 1893 World's Fair. *Harvard Gazette,* https://news.harvard.edu/gazette/story/2018/08/rare-portraits -from-chicago-worlds-fair-of-1893-spark-new-research/

Tatum, B. D. (1997). *Why are all the Black kids sitting together in the cafeteria? And other conversations about race.* Basic Books.

Theimer, C. E., Killen, M., & Stangor, C. (2001). Young children's evaluations of exclusion in gender-stereotypic peer contexts. *Developmental Psychology, 37*(1), 18–27.

Thompson, L. A., & Qualls, S. (Illustrator). (2015). *Emmanuel's dream: The true story of Emmanuel Ofosu Yeboah.* Random House.

Tyson, C. A. (2003). A bridge over troubled water: Social studies, civic education, and critical race theory. In G. Ladson-Billings (Ed.), *Critical race theory perspectives on the social studies: The profession, policies, and curriculum* (pp. 15–25). Information Age.

U.S. Constitution. (1787). *Preamble.* https://avalon.law.yale.edu/18th_century/usconst.asp

Uchida, Y., & Yardley, J. (1996). *The bracelet.* Puffin Books.

Ulrich, L. T. (1990). *A midwife's tale: The life of Martha Ballard, based on her diary, 1785–1812.* Alfred Knopf.

VanSledright, B. A. (2006). Clearing the water? A difficult task of balancing aims and rationales in social education. *Theory & Research in Social Education, 34*(3), 408–415.

VanSledright, B. A. (2008). Narratives of nation-state, historical knowledge, and school history education. *Review of Research in Education, 32*(1), 109–146.

VanSledright, B. A. (2011). *The challenge of rethinking history education: On practices, theories, and policy.* Taylor & Francis.

VanSledright, B. A., & Afflerbach, P. (2000). Reconstructing Andrew Jackson: Prospective elementary teachers' readings of revisionist history texts. *Theory & Research in Social Education, 28*(3), 411–444.

VanSledright, B. A., & Brophy, J. (1992). Storytelling, imagination, and fanciful elaboration in children's historical reconstructions. *American Educational Research Journal, 29*(4), 837–859.

Varelas, M., Martin, D. B., & Kane, J. M. (2012). Content learning and identity construction: A framework to strengthen African American students' mathematics and science learning in urban elementary schools. *Human Development, 55*(5–6), 319–339.

Vinson, K. D. (2001). Oppression, anti-oppression, and citizenship education. In E. W. Ross (Ed.), *The social studies curriculum: Purposes, problems, and possibilities* (Vol. 2, pp. 57–85). State University of New York Press.

Vygotsky, L. S. (1978). *Mind in society: The development of higher psychological processes.* Harvard University Press.

Wade, R. C. (2007). *Social studies for social justice: Teaching strategies for the elementary classroom.* Teachers College Press.

Washington Post & Social Science Research Solutions. (2019). *July 1–7, 2019, Washington Post-SSRS poll.* https://www.washingtonpost.com/context/july-1-7-2019-washington-post-ssrs-poll/54e83dcc-32bb-4d8b-9cff-ae8da8342642/

Wertsch, J. V. (1998). *Mind as action.* Oxford University Press.

Wertsch, J. V. (2000). Is it possible to teach beliefs, as well as knowledge about history? In P. N. Stearns, P. C. Seixas, & S. S. Wineburg (Eds.), *Knowing, teaching, and learning history: National and international perspectives* (pp. 38–50). New York University Press.

Wertsch, J. V. (2002). *Voices of collective remembering.* Cambridge University Press.

Wertsch, J. V. (2008a). Collective memory and narrative templates. *Social Research: An International Quarterly, 75*(1), 133–156.

Wertsch, J. V. (2008b). The narrative organization of collective memory. *Ethos, 36*(1), 120–135.

Wertsch, J. V. (2012). Deep memory and narrative templates: Conservative forces in collective memory. In A. Assmann & L. Shortt (Eds.), *Memory and political change* (pp. 173–185). Springer.

Wertsch, J. V., & O'Connor, K. (1994). Multivoicedness in historical representation: American college students' accounts of the origins of the United States. *Journal of Narrative and Life History, 4*(4), 295–309.

Westheimer, J. (2015). *What kind of citizen? Educating our children for the common good*. Teachers College Press.

Westheimer, J., & Kahne, J. (2004). What kind of citizen? The politics of educating for democracy. *American Educational Research Journal, 41*(2), 237–269.

Wineburg, S. S. (1991a). Historical problem solving: A study of the cognitive processes used in the evaluation of documentary and pictorial evidence. *Journal of Educational Psychology, 83*(1), 73–87.

Wineburg, S. S. (1991b). On the reading of historical texts: Notes on the breach between school and academy. *American Educational Research Journal, 28*(3), 495–519.

Wineburg, S. S. (1999). Historical thinking and other unnatural acts. *Phi Delta Kappan, 80*(7), 488–489.

Wineburg, S. S. (2001). *Historical thinking and other unnatural acts: Charting the future of teaching the past*. Temple University Press.

Wineburg, S. S. (2016). Why historical thinking is not about history. *History News*, 13–16.

Wineburg, S. S. (2018). *Why learn history (When it's already on your phone)*. University of Chicago Press.

Wineburg, S. S., & Reisman, A. (2015). Disciplinary literacy in history: A toolkit for digital citizenship. *Journal of Adolescent & Adult Literacy, 58*(8), 636–639.

Woodson, A. N. (2015). "What you supposed to know": Urban Black students' perspectives on history textbooks. *Journal of Urban Learning, Teaching, and Research, 11*(1), 57–65.

Woodson, A. N. (2016). We're just ordinary people: Messianic master narratives and Black youths' civic agency. *Theory & Research in Social Education, 44*(2), 184–211.

Woodson, A. N. (2017). "There ain't no White people here": Master narratives of the civil rights movement in the stories of urban youth. *Urban Education, 52*(3), 316–342.

Woodson, A. N., & Duncan, K. E. (2018). When keeping it real goes wrong: Race talk, racial blunders, and redemption. In C. C. Martell (Ed.), *Social studies teacher education: Critical issues and current perspectives* (pp. 101–112). Information Age.

Woodward, A. (1987). Textbooks: Less than meets the eye. *Journal of Curriculum Studies, 19*(6), 511–526.

Woyshner, C. (2002). Political history as women's history: Toward a more inclusive curriculum. *Theory & Research in Social Education, 30*(3), 354–380.

Yeager, E. A., & Wilson, E. K. (1997). Teaching historical thinking in the social studies methods course: A case study. *The Social Studies, 88*(3), 121–126.

Zinn, H. (1990). *The politics of history* (2nd ed.). University of Illinois Press.

Zinn, H. (2002). *You can't be neutral on a moving train: A personal history of our times*. Beacon Press.

Zinn, H. (2002, September 18). *Q&A in Albuquerque*. Alternative Radio. https://www.alternativeradio.org/products/zinh047/

Zinn, H. (2003). *A people's history of the United States*. Harper Perennial. (Original work published 1980)

Zinn, H. (2009). *The Zinn reader: Writings on disobedience and democracy*. Seven Stories Press. (Original work published 1997)

About the Authors and Contributors

Christopher C. Martell is an assistant professor at the University of Massachusetts Boston. He teaches courses on elementary and secondary social studies methods. He was a high school social studies teacher for 11 years, including 8 years in the Framingham Public Schools, an urban district west of Boston. Before joining UMass Boston, he was a professor at Boston University. Chris is the editor of the book *Social Studies Teacher Education: Critical Issues and Current Perspectives*. His research and scholarly work have been featured in numerous peer-reviewed books and journals, including the *Journal of Teacher Education, Teaching and Teacher Education, Theory & Research in Social Education*, and *Social Education*. His scholarship and professional interests center on teacher development across the career span, including preservice teacher preparation, inservice professional development, and practitioner inquiry. He is particularly interested in social studies teachers in urban and multicultural contexts, critical race theory, culturally relevant/sustaining pedagogy, and historical inquiry. He has a bachelor's degree in history from the University of Massachusetts Amherst, master's degree in curriculum and instruction from Boston College, and a doctorate in curriculum and teaching from Boston University.

Kaylene M. Stevens is a lecturer at Boston University Wheelock College of Education & Human Development. She teaches courses on historical literacy, research methods, and elementary and secondary social studies methods. Prior to her work at Boston University, she was a high school teacher at Framingham High School for 14 years and department chair for the Social Studies Department for 4 years. At Framingham, she was also the director of Step Up to Excellence, a mentoring program for youth of low socioeconomic status, and led the new teacher program for the high school. She has authored several publications on gender-equitable and race-conscious teaching in the social studies classroom. Her work has been featured in *Theory & Research in Social Education* and the *Journal of Social Studies Research*. Her research and professional interests focus on gender equity in the social studies classroom, race-conscious teaching for social studies, and culturally relevant pedagogy and curriculum. She has a bachelor's degree in sociology from Hamilton College, master's degree in teaching from Union College, and a doctorate in curriculum and teaching from Boston University.

Neema Avashia is an 8th-grade civics teacher in the Boston Public Schools, where she has taught for the last 16 years. She was born and raised in Cross Lanes, West Virginia, to Indian immigrant parents. She completed undergraduate studies at Carnegie Mellon University, and has master's degrees in education policy studies from the University of Wisconsin Madison and teaching from the University of Massachusetts Boston.

Jennifer R. Bryson is a former classroom teacher in the Chelsea Public Schools. She specializes in the professional preparation of elementary education teachers. She currently serves as the program director for elementary education and the faculty director for educator preparation at Boston University's Wheelock College of Education and Human Development. She grew up in Queens, New York. She has a bachelor's degree in elementary education, master's degree in literacy and language, and doctorate in literacy and developmental studies from Boston University.

Taylor Collins is a social studies teacher at Framingham High School in Framingham, Massachusetts, where she teaches U.S. history. She has taught for 13 years in total, with 4 years in North Carolina. As a North Carolina native, she graduated from Appalachian (a-puh-la-chn) State University with a bachelor's degree in history and secondary education, and a master's degree in curriculum and instruction from Boston College.

Maria R. Sequenzia is a social studies teacher at Framingham High School in Framingham, Massachusetts. This is her 15th year there; she currently teaches AP U.S. history, modern world history, and AP psychology. She grew up in Connecticut. She received her bachelor's degree in politics and psychology from Mount Holyoke College and her master's degree in education from Harvard University.

Index